studysync®

Reading & Writing Companion

Uncovering Truth

How do challenges cause us to reveal our true selves?

studysync®

studysync.com

Send all inquiries to:
BookheadEd Learning, LLC
610 Daniel Young Drive
Sonoma, CA 95476

ISBN 978-1-94-973911-4

3 4 5 6 LMN 24 23 22 21 20

B

Student Guide

Getting Started

Welcome to the StudySync Reading & Writing Companion! In this book, you will find a collection of readings based on the theme of the unit you are studying. As you work through the readings, you will be asked to answer questions and perform a variety of tasks designed to help you closely analyze and understand each text selection. Read on for an explanation of each section of this book.

Close Reading and Writing Routine

In each unit, you will read texts that share a common theme, despite their different genres, time periods, and authors. Each reading encourages a closer look through questions and a short writing assignment.

1

Introduction

An Introduction to each text provides historical context for your reading as well as information about the author. You will also learn about the genre of the text and the year in which it was written.

2

Notes

Many times, while working through the activities after each text, you will be asked to **annotate** or **make annotations** about what you are reading. This means that you should highlight or underline words in the text and use the "Notes" column to make comments or jot down any questions you have. You may also want to note any unfamiliar vocabulary words here.

You will also see sample student annotations to go along with the Skill lesson for that text.

Are the New 'Golden Age' TV Shows the New Novels?

INFORMATIONAL TEXT
Adam Kirsch and Mohsin Hamid
2014

Introduction   study SYNC ®

Adam Kirsch (b. 1976) is a magazine editor, educator, and poet. He is also a literary critic, winning the Roger Shattuck Prize for Criticism in 2010. Mohsin Hamid (b. 1971) is a novelist, known best for *The Reluctant Fundamentalist*, *Exit West*, and his PEN/Hemingway Award finalist *Moth Smoke*. In this op-ed essay from the *New York Times*, both writers share their thoughts on how contemporary TV has changed how we think about the novel. Through a discussion of the style of Charles Dickens' writing, and an examination of novelistic features, both authors present persuasive arguments for their answer to the question "Are the New 'Golden Age' TV Shows the New Novels?"

Are the New 'Golden Age' TV Shows the New Novels?

> To liken TV shows
> to novels suggests an odd
> ambivalence toward both genres.

By Adam Kirsch

One criticism that could be leveled against quality cable TV is that it is not nearly as formally adventurous as Dickens himself.

1   Television was so bad for so long, it's no surprise that the arrival of good television has caused the culture to lose its head a bit. Since the debut of "The Sopranos" in 1999, we have been living, so we are regularly informed, in a "golden age" of television. And over the last few years, it's become common to hear variations on the idea that quality cable TV shows are the new novels. Thomas Doherty, writing in *The Chronicle of Higher Education*, called the new genre "Arc TV"—because its stories follow long, complex arcs of development—and insisted that "at its best, the world of Arc TV is as exquisitely calibrated as the social matrix of a Henry James novel."

2   To liken TV shows to novels suggests an odd **ambivalence** toward both genres. Clearly, the comparison is intended to honor TV, by associating it with the prestige and complexity that traditionally belong to literature. But at the same time, it is covertly a form of aggression against literature, suggesting that novels have ceded their role to a younger, more popular, more dynamic art form. Mixed feelings about literature—the desire to annex its virtues while simultaneously belittling them—are typical of our culture today, which doesn't know quite how to deal with an art form, like the novel, that is both democratic and demanding.

3   It's not surprising that the novelist most often mentioned in this context is Charles Dickens. Dickens, like Shakespeare, was both a writer of genius and a popular entertainer, proving that seriousness of purpose didn't preclude accessibility. His novels appeared in serial installments, like episodes of TV

Skill:
Textual Evidence

Before 1999, television was generally lower quality than the innovative television shows after 1999. The pre-1999 shows did not follow complex story arcs throughout a season the way that a novel does from start to finish.

Reading & Writing Companion

3 First Read

During your first reading of each selection, you should just try to get a general idea of the content and message of the reading. Don't worry if there are parts you don't understand or words that are unfamiliar to you. You'll have an opportunity later to dive deeper into the text.

4 Think Questions

These questions will ask you to start thinking critically about the text, asking specific questions about its purpose, and making connections to your prior knowledge and reading experiences. To answer these questions, you should go back to the text and draw upon specific evidence to support your responses. You will also begin to explore some of the more challenging vocabulary words in the selection.

5 Skills

Each Skill includes two parts: Checklist and Your Turn. In the Checklist, you will learn the process for analyzing the text. The model student annotations in the text provide examples of how you might make your own notes following the instructions in the Checklist. In the Your Turn, you will use those same instructions to practice the skill.

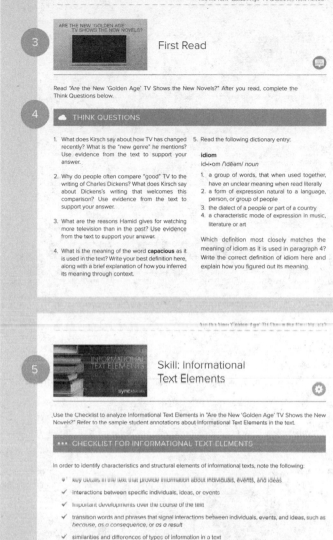

3 First Read

Read "Are the New 'Golden Age' TV Shows the New Novels?" After you read, complete the Think Questions below.

4 THINK QUESTIONS

1. What does Kirsch say about how TV has changed recently? What is the "new genre" he mentions? Use evidence from the text to support your answer.

2. Why do people often compare "good" TV to the writing of Charles Dickens? What does Kirsch say about Dickens's writing that welcomes this comparison? Use evidence from the text to support your answer.

3. What are the reasons Hamid gives for watching more television than in the past? Use evidence from the text to support your answer.

4. What is the meaning of the word **capacious** as it is used in the text? Write your best definition here, along with a brief explanation of how you inferred its meaning through context.

5. Read the following dictionary entry:

idiom
id·i·om /ˈidēəm/ *noun*

1. a group of words, that when used together, have an unclear meaning when read literally
2. a form of expression natural to a language, person, or group of people
3. the dialect of a people or part of a country
4. a characteristic mode of expression in music, literature or art

Which definition most closely matches the meaning of idiom as it is used in paragraph 4? Write the correct definition of idiom here and explain how you figured out its meaning.

5 Skill: Informational Text Elements

Use the Checklist to analyze Informational Text Elements in "Are the New 'Golden Age' TV Shows the New Novels?" Refer to the sample student annotations about Informational Text Elements in the text.

CHECKLIST FOR INFORMATIONAL TEXT ELEMENTS

In order to identify characteristics and structural elements of informational texts, note the following:

- ✓ key details in the text that provide information about individuals, events, and ideas
- ✓ interactions between specific individuals, ideas, or events
- ✓ important developments over the course of the text
- ✓ transition words and phrases that signal interactions between individuals, events, and ideas, such as *because, as a consequence,* or *as a result*
- ✓ similarities and differences of types of information in a text

To analyze a complex set of ideas or sequence of events and explain how specific

- ✓ individuals, ideas, or events interact and develop over the course of the text, consider the following questions:
- ✓ How does the author present the information as a sequence of events?
- ✓ How does the order in which ideas or events are presented affect the connections between them?
- ✓ How do specific individuals, ideas, or events interact and develop over the course of the text?
- ✓ What other features, if any, help readers to analyze the events, ideas, or individuals in the text?

YOUR TURN

1. What does the author's use of the transition phrase "for instance" tell the reader?

   - ○ A. that the sentence includes an example to support the idea in the sentence before it
   - ○ B. that the sentence includes an example to support the idea in the sentence after it
   - ○ C. that the author's main point in the paragraph is explained in the sentence.
   - ○ D. that the second half of the paragraph discusses a new topic

2. Why does the author compare Gilbert Osmond to Tony Soprano in paragraph 5?

   - ○ A. to conclude that Soprano is a more likeable character than Osmond
   - ○ B. to show a counterexample to his thesis that he then refutes
   - ○ C. to give clear and concrete evidence to support his thesis
   - ○ D. to refer to a character in a novel that all Americans have read

ARE THE NEW 'GOLDEN AGE' TV SHOWS THE NEW NOVELS?

Close Read

6

Reread "Are the New 'Golden Age' TV Shows the New Novels?" As you reread, complete the Skills Focus questions below. Then use your answers and annotations from the questions to help you complete the Write activity.

◎ SKILLS FOCUS

1. What are the advantages and disadvantages of how TV shows are structured? Use textual evidence to support your answer.

2. Mohsin Hamid believes that TV shows pose a real threat for novelists, and that novelists will need to find a way to adapt in the future. How does Hamid structure his argument?

3. Highlight two examples of supporting evidence in Kirsch's essay. How does the author connect these pieces of evidence to other parts of his argument?

4. Although the authors have different ideas about the role of literature in our lives, they both see a future for both novels and TV shows. What direction would each author give to these artforms? Highlight and annotate examples from the text to support your answer.

✎ WRITE

7

EXPLANATORY ESSAY: Select one of the articles. Analyze how the author uses examples, explanations, and concluding remarks to support his thesis and provide direction to his ideas. Remember to use textual evidence to support your points.

Fate or Foolishness

FICTION

Introduction

A n accident creates a violent element that threatens the planet. Can a human and a computerized bird restore things to normal?

▣ VOCABULARY

chasm
a deep crack in the surface of the earth

bizarre
extremely strange or odd

collide
to crash together violently

ominous
threatening; suggesting that something bad will happen

---

6 Close Read & Skills Focus

After you have completed the First Read, you will be asked to go back and read the text more closely and critically. Before you begin your Close Read, you should read through the Skills Focus to get an idea of the concepts you will want to focus on during your second reading. You should work through the Skills Focus by making annotations, highlighting important concepts, and writing notes or questions in the "Notes" column. Depending on instructions from your teacher, you may need to respond online or use a separate piece of paper to start expanding on your thoughts and ideas.

7 Write

Your study of each selection will end with a writing assignment. For this assignment, you should use your notes, annotations, personal ideas, and answers to both the Think and Skills Focus questions. Be sure to read the prompt carefully and address each part of it in your writing.

8 English Language Learner

The English Language Learner texts focus on improving language proficiency. You will practice learning strategies and skills in individual and group activities to become better readers, writers, and speakers.

Extended Writing Project and Grammar

This is your opportunity to use genre characteristics and craft to compose meaningful, longer written works exploring the theme of each unit. You will draw information from your readings, research, and own life experiences to complete the assignment.

1 Writing Project

After you have read all of the unit text selections, you will move on to a writing project. Each project will guide you through the process of writing your essay. Student models will provide guidance and help you organize your thoughts. One unit ends with an **Extended Oral Project** which will give you an opportunity to develop your oral language and communication skills.

2 Writing Process Steps

There are four steps in the writing process: Plan, Draft, Revise, and Edit and Publish. During each step, you will form and shape your writing project, and each lesson's peer review will give you the chance to receive feedback from your peers and teacher.

3 Writing Skills

Each Skill lesson focuses on a specific strategy or technique that you will use during your writing project. Each lesson presents a process for applying the skill to your own work and gives you the opportunity to practice it to improve your writing.

1 Extended Writing Project and Grammar

Extended Writing Project and Grammar

2 Informative Writing Process: Plan

| PLAN | DRAFT | REVISE | EDIT AND PUBLISH |

Extended Writing Project and Grammar

3 Skill: Organizing Informative Writing

••• CHECKLIST FOR ORGANIZING INFORMATIVE WRITING

As you begin to organize your writing for your informative essay, use the following questions as a guide:

• What is a brief summary of my topic?
• How can I organize my ideas so that each new element builds on previous material?
• Can I use visual elements, such as headings, to organize my essay by dividing information into sections?

Here are steps you can use to organize complex ideas, concepts, and information so that each new element builds on that which precedes it to create a unified whole:

Uncovering Truth

How do challenges cause us to reveal our true selves?

Genre Focus: **FICTION**

Texts

🔗 Paired Readings

Extended Writing Project and Grammar

English Language Learner Resources

Unit 2: Uncovering Truth
How do challenges cause us to reveal our true selves?

SIMON ARMITAGE

Simon Armitage (b. 1963) has written poems, novels, plays, and even a script for a puppet opera. He published his critically-acclaimed translation of the 14th-century Arthurian chivalric poem, *Sir Gawain and the Green Knight,* in 2008, which has sold over 100,000 copies worldwide. Originally written in alliterative verse, its author remains unknown. Armitage, who was elected to serve as Professor of Poetry at Oxford, has also taught at the University of Leeds and the University of Iowa's Writer's Workshop.

BILL BRYSON

Born in Iowa, Bill Bryson (b. 1951) has lived in Britain since the 1970s, when he decided to move there following a four-month backpacking trip of Europe. A trained journalist, he has written a number of popular nonfiction books on subjects ranging from travel to science to language. His 2007 biography of William Shakespeare investigates some of the controversies surrounding the playwright and poet, such as the well-rehearsed authorship debate.

GEOFFREY CHAUCER

Known as the first English author, Geoffrey Chaucer (c. 1343–1400) elected to write in English, the language of the lower-class Saxons, when Latin was commonly spoken and the aristocracy spoke mainly in French. The son of a middle-class wine merchant and a squire in the court of Elizabeth, Countess of Ulster, Chaucer was attentive to subtle class distinctions, which was often the basis of his stories. His best-known work, *The Canterbury Tales* (1387), has an innovative form, distinguished by the wide-ranging social ranks of its characters.

T. S. ELIOT

One of the most highly regarded poets of his time, T. S. Eliot (1888–1965) was also a playwright and an influential literary critic. In his 1919 essay on Shakespeare's *Hamlet*, he put forward his concept of the "objective correlative"—a set of objects, a situation, or a chain of events that evokes a certain emotion in an audience. When asked in a *Paris Review* interview about the difference between plays and poems, Eliot replied, "There is all the difference in the world between writing a play for an audience and writing a poem, in which you're writing primarily for yourself."

SHAQUEM GRIFFIN

NFL football player Shaquem Griffin (b. 1995) overcame major obstacles on his journey to becoming a professional football player. Born with a congenital illness that prevented his left hand from fully developing, he often faced discrimination from other players and coaches. He penned an open letter to the general managers of the NFL in 2018 about his experiences fighting adversity. Several weeks later, he was selected in the 2018 NFL Draft by the Seattle Seahawks.

SEAMUS HEANEY

Poet, scholar, and translator, Seamus Heaney (1939–2013) grew up a Catholic in Protestant Northern Ireland. Though he would later live in Dublin for many years, the often-violent political conflict that surrounded him in his youth was at the core of much of his writing. Heaney published over twenty volumes of poetry and criticism and several anthologies, but is perhaps best known for his translation of the epic Anglo-Saxon poem *Beowulf*. Heaney's translation of this foundational Old English text is groundbreaking for its use of modern language.

GARETH HINDS

Illustrator Gareth Hinds (b. 1971) has adapted numerous literary classics into critically-acclaimed graphic novels. His rendition of Beowulf, written by an unknown Anglo-Saxon poet around the 10th or 11th century, dramatically depicts a series of epic battles featuring the hero Beowulf. *A Publishers Weekly* reviewer describes Hinds's perspectives and palettes as lending the book "an almost overwhelming sense of menace."

NAOMI SHIHAB NYE

After the World Trade Center attacks in 2001, writer Naomi Shihab Nye (b. 1952) became an active advocate for Arab Americans, voicing her opposition to both terrorism and prejudice. Her 2005 book, *You & Yours*, was divided into sections addressing her personal experience as a mother and traveler and conditions in the Middle East. Born in St. Louis and raised in both San Antonio, Texas, and Jerusalem, Nye focuses on cultural difference, local life, and the everyday in her work, which spans poetry, fiction, essays, and translations.

WILLIAM SHAKESPEARE

William Shakespeare (1564–1616) is widely regarded as the greatest playwright of all time. His work, which coincided in large part with the reign of England's Queen Elizabeth I, came to define that period in literary history. In addition to comedies and tragedies, he also wrote plays based on major events in English history. *Richard III*, the last in a sequence of four plays set in the late 14th and early 15th centuries, opens with a soliloquy in which Richard discloses his plans to seize the throne through murder, lies, and betrayal.

RABINDRANATH TAGORE

A native of Calcutta, India, Rabindranath Tagore (1861–1941) was the first non-European to win the Nobel Prize in Literature, in 1913. His numerous novels, stories, plays, songs, and poems were influenced by both Western modernism and Indian storytelling traditions, and he is known for introducing colloquial language into Bengali literature. His frequent encounters with the village folk in present-day Bangladesh, where he lived for ten years, formed the basis for much of his later writing.

JESMYN WARD

A native of the Mississippi Gulf Coast, Jesmyn Ward (b. 1977) experienced Hurricane Katrina first hand. This devastating event features prominently in her work, especially her 2011 novel, *Salvage the Bones*, as a focal point for broader inquiries into race and class struggles. Her complex characters and poetic language reflect the depth of experience that constitutes life along the Gulf Coast.

The Medieval Period

Introduction

This informational text provides readers with background information about the history and culture of medieval literature, focusing on the intricacies of the societies that gave rise to heroes like Beowulf, Sir Gawain, and King Arthur. Readers will explore some of the earliest written works of the English language, including epic poetry and medieval romances. For those interested in the earliest foundations of modern epic heroes like Black Panther or Tris Prior, this introduction to medieval literature explains the context in which many of our classic folk heroes and romances first came to be.

"The epic hero almost always defeats his enemies."

1   What are some of your favorite movies? Do any of these movies tell the story of an amazing hero with superhuman abilities? There have been many recent blockbusters about extraordinary heroes like Black Panther, Tris Prior, and Harry Potter—to name a few. These modern-day heroes are part of a long lineage of heroes and legends celebrated in literature throughout history and across cultures. Traveling back all the way to the English Middle Ages we find Beowulf, an Anglo-Saxon warrior, and King Arthur, a legendary medieval king   heroic figures who still capture our imagination and remain **relevant** in today's entertainment Industry.

Anglo-Saxon Warriors

2   The English Middle Ages ranged from the end of the fifth century to 1485. The Romans had conquered Britain, but they left when the Roman Empire began to fall. Meanwhile, invaders from a mix of tribes from Germany, Denmark, and the Netherlands came to Britain in ships across the North Sea. The three biggest tribes were the Angles, the Saxons, and the Jutes, and today they are collectively referred to as the **Anglo-Saxons.**

3   The Anglo-Saxons brought their language, culture, and literary traditions to Britain. Anglo-Saxon storytellers created heroic songs describing warriors' great deeds and celebrating qualities such as strength, courage, and loyalty. Minstrels performed these songs during banquets in the mead-halls of Anglo-Saxon rulers. In a mostly illiterate society, such songs served as entertainment. They also provided models for warriors to emulate and a goal to pursue— namely, to win fame and be remembered after death for one's deeds. During this period, an unknown poet composed *Beowulf,* the oldest known **epic** poem in England.

Christianity and Pilgrimages

4   In 596 CE Pope Gregory I sent missionaries to convert the Anglo-Saxons to Christianity. By 650 CE, most of England was Christian, though many people retained some pagan beliefs and traditions. One way people expressed their religious devotion during the Middle Ages was to undertake a pilgrimage, or journey to a sacred site. One of the most important destinations for English

Please note that excerpts and passages in the StudySync® library and this workbook are intended as touchstones to generate interest in an author's work. The excerpts and passages do not substitute for the reading of entire texts, and StudySync® strongly recommends that students seek out and purchase the whole literary or informational work in order to experience it as the author intended. Links to online resellers are available in our digital library. In addition, complete works may be ordered through an authorized reseller by filling out and returning to StudySync® the order form enclosed in this workbook.

Reading & Writing Companion   1

pilgrims was Canterbury Cathedral. In fact, the pilgrims described in Chaucer's *The Canterbury Tales* are journeying to this holy site.

Knights and Chivalry

5   The Anglo-Saxon era ended in 1066 when William the Conqueror landed with his army in England and attacked and defeated the Anglo-Saxons to become the first Norman king of England. The Normans introduced the system of **feudalism**, under which land was divided among the nobility. Knights pledged their wealth and services to barons, who in turn provided use of the land. Constant warfare in the Middle Ages involved troops of heavily armed knights fighting each other. Given their role in society, knights enjoyed great social prestige in the feudal aristocracy system. It was during this time period that English writers produced romances about the legendary King Arthur and his Knights of the Round Table, with *Sir Gawain and the Green Knight* as one of the most highly regarded verse romances in English.

William I, King of England, also known as William the Conqueror

Major Concepts

6   • **Anglo-Saxon virtues**—Anglo-Saxon culture was a warrior society. They were under constant attack, such as during the Viking raids of the eighth and ninth centuries. Courage, loyalty, and physical strength were important virtues and through them it was believed that a warrior could achieve fame and immortality.

   • **The Power of Faith**—The Christian church shaped the culture of medieval England, influencing all aspects of life: politics, warfare, education, business, art, literature, folkways, and recreation.

NOTES

- **Code of Chivalry**—During the time period of feudalism, knights enjoyed a high social status and were expected to exhibit exemplary behavior. The code of **chivalry,** an ideal of civilized behavior among the nobility, encouraged knights to be honorable, generous, brave, skillful in battle, and respectful to women.

Style and Form

Epic Poetry

7 - *Beowulf* is considered an epic poem—a long narrative poem that recounts the **exploits** of a larger-than-life hero. It is characterized by poetic lines with regular meter and formal, lofty language.

- The earliest epics date back to a time when most people were illiterate. These epics were recited by poets and likely included musical accompaniment.

- Epic plots typically involve supernatural events, long periods of time, distant journeys, and life-and-death struggles between good and evil.

- The epic hero is a man—women take a subordinate role in traditional epics—of high social status whose fate affects the destiny of his people. He embodies the ideals and values of his people. Through physical strength, skill as a warrior, nobility of character, and quick wits, the epic hero almost always defeats his enemies.

A Collection of Tales

8 - In a collection of tales, several stories are framed by a larger story. A collection is not specific to writing in the medieval period. It is a traditional storytelling form that has been used by cultures worldwide.

- Geoffrey Chaucer's *The Canterbury Tales* is a well-known collection, which is highly representative of medieval culture and values. In *The Canterbury Tales*, the larger story frame is that of a group of pilgrims. Each tale is an individual story told by one of the pilgrims.

- Chaucer's tales are written mostly in verse, although some are in prose.

- Chaucer's characters represent a diversity of views as well as different social classes.

Medieval Romance

9 - *Sir Gawain and the Green Knight* is a medieval romance. **Medieval romances** often told romantic tales about legendary heroes, such as King Arthur and his knights. They were written in both verse and prose. The

Please note that excerpts and passages in the StudySync® library and this workbook are intended as touchstones to generate interest in an author's work. The excerpts and passages do not substitute for the reading of entire texts, and StudySync® strongly recommends that students seek out and purchase the whole literary or informational work in order to experience it as the author intended. Links to online resellers are available in our digital library. In addition, complete works may be ordered through an authorized reseller by filling out and returning to StudySync® the order form enclosed in this workbook.

Reading & Writing Companion   3

emphasis on chivalry and courtly love distinguishes medieval romance from other types of epics.

- Romance was the most popular literary genre in medieval England among the upper classes.

- The knight usually goes on a quest and in the course of his adventures, undergoes a process of self-discovery and self-improvement.

- The romance hero follows a strict code of conduct, demonstrating absolute loyalty to his king and an unwavering adherence to his oaths as well as exhibiting courtly manners toward women and protecting and aiding the defenseless.

The Knight's Progress of Arthurian Legend

10 Epic poems, medieval romances, and pilgrims' tales were the movies of their day. Audiences were enthralled by stories of epic warriors, legendary knights, courtly love, supernatural monsters, perilous journeys, and fierce battles. Epic poems, romances, and folk tales have continued to captivate readers throughout literary history. Where do you notice the influence of medieval literature on today's films and literature?

LITERARY FOCUS:
THE MEDIEVAL PERIOD

Literary Focus

Read "Literary Focus: The Medieval Period." After you read, complete the Think Questions below.

☁ THINK QUESTIONS

1. What specific themes, characters, and plot points might audiences of medieval literature find in a typical epic poem or medieval romance? Cite evidence from the text as support.

2. What were the expectations of knights in medieval times? Why do you think they were expected to behave this way? Explain, citing textual evidence to support your response.

3. How did the fact that Anglo-Saxon society was largely illiterate affect entertainment during this time period? Explain.

4. Use context clues to determine the meaning of the word **chivalry** as it is used in this text. Write your definition here, along with the words and phrases that were most helpful in coming to your conclusion. Finally, consult a dictionary to confirm your understanding.

5. The word **exploit** has multiple meanings. Use a print or digital resource to clarify and validate which meaning is used in this text. Cite any context clues that were helpful in determining the word's meaning.

Beowulf
(A Graphic Novel)

FICTION
Gareth Hinds
2007

Introduction

Gareth Hinds (b. 1971) has adapted numerous literary classics into graphic novel form, including *Beowulf*, an epic poem written in Old English and widely considered to be the most important and enduring work of Old English literature. Though its origin date is contested amongst scholars, a first manuscript is widely believed to have been created sometime between 970 and 1025 A.D. The poem was written by an Anglo-Saxon of unknown identity, but the story itself is set firmly in the Scandinavia of yore. The tale follows the heroic journey of Beowulf, who comes to the aid of a king to defeat the murderous monster, Grendel. In this excerpt, Beowulf confronts the gigantic creature.

"Therefore I shall carry neither sword nor shield nor coat of mail to this battle."

Panel 1

NOTES

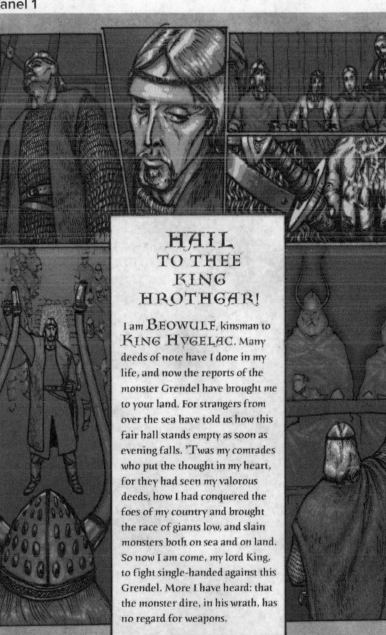

HAIL
TO THEE
KING
HROTHGAR!

I am BEOWULF, kinsman to KING HYGELAC. Many deeds of note have I done in my life, and now the reports of the monster Grendel have brought me to your land. For strangers from over the sea have told us how this fair hall stands empty as soon as evening falls. 'Twas my comrades who put the thought in my heart, for they had seen my valorous deeds, how I had conquered the foes of my country and brought the race of giants low, and slain monsters both on sea and on land. So now I am come, my lord King, to fight single-handed against this Grendel. More I have heard: that the monster dire, in his wrath, has no regard for weapons.

Panel 2

Therefore I shall carry neither sword nor shield nor coat of mail to this battle. With the grip of my hands only will I confront this enemy, struggling with him, life for life. But who shall live and who shall die, let it be as God shall will.

I DOUBT NOT, O King, that if he has his way, he will devour the champions of the Geats, even as he has those of the Danes. As for me, thou wilt not need to lay my body in the earth and raise a mound over it, for he will surely carry it off to the moors where he dwells and devour it there. Only I pray thee to send back to King Hygelac my armor, for it came to me by inheritance, and Wayland, the smith of the gods, wrought it in the old time. But that which Fate has ordered shall come to pass.

Panel 3

NOTES

NOTES

Panel 4

Art thou that Beowulf who contended with Breca in swimming on the open sea? 'Twas indeed foolhardy, yet no man could turn you from your adventure. Seven days and nights ye toiled, one against the other, but in the end he prevailed, for he had the greater strength.
The waves cast him ashore on the land of the Hearthoram, whence he journeyed back to his own kingdom. So I predict a worse adventure for thee – though doubtless thou art a sturdy warrior in the shock of battle – if thou dare to await Grendel's coming through the watch of night.

Panel 5

Surely the ale-can has wrought with thee, friend Unferth, that thou hast said such things about Breca. But I say to thee that in buffeting the waves of the sea, I have more strength than any man under heaven.

Now hear the truth. This Breca and I, in our boyhood, were wont to talk of this — how we would test ourselves against the sea — and we made agreement to contend one against the other. So we swam, each holding in one hand a sword to defend himself against the monsters of the sea. Not one whit farther than I could he swim, nor could I outpace him.

So for the space of five days and nights we swam together, but on the sixth day the floods parted us, for the wind blew mightily from the north and the waves were rough. So was I left alone, and the rage of the sea-monsters was roused against me; but my coat of mail stood me in good stead against their attacks. In grimmest grip did one great beast seize me and drag me to the bottom of the sea. Yet strength was given me to pierce the monster with my sword, and I slew him.

---

1. **Breca** a close, childhood friend of Beowulf

Panel 6

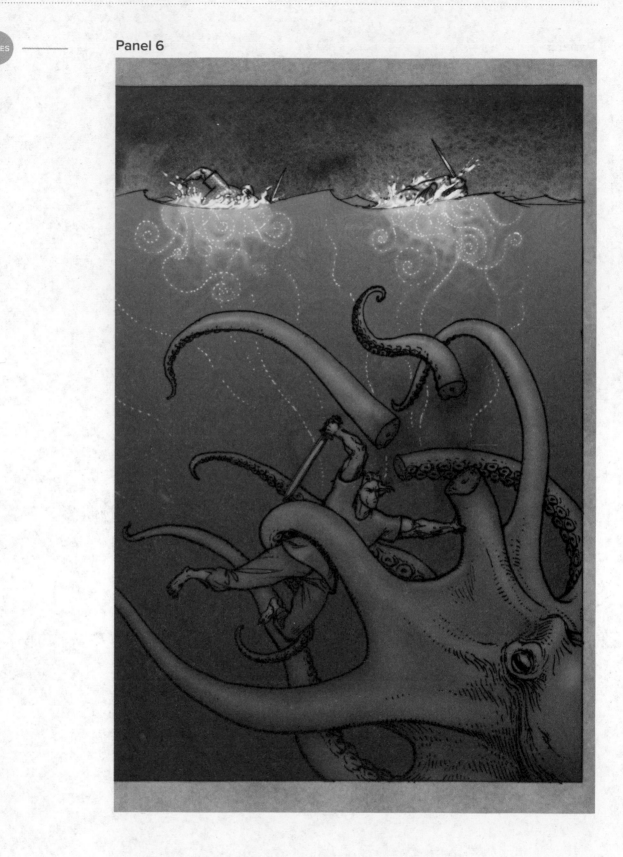

Panel 7

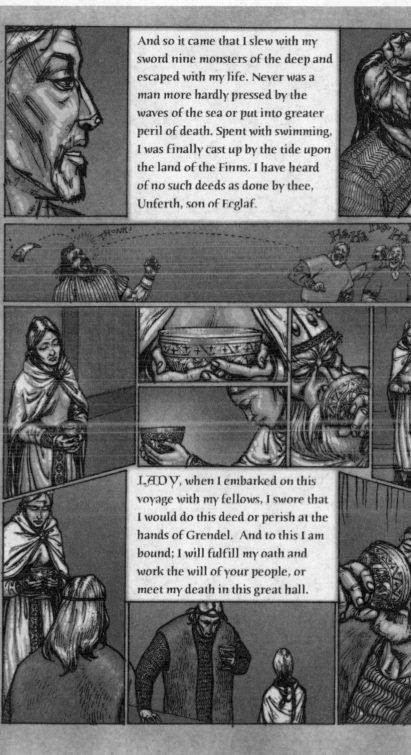

And so it came that I slew with my sword nine monsters of the deep and escaped with my life. Never was a man more hardly pressed by the waves of the sea or put into greater peril of death. Spent with swimming, I was finally cast up by the tide upon the land of the Finns. I have heard of no such deeds as done by thee, Unferth, son of Ecglaf.

LADY, when I embarked on this voyage with my fellows, I swore that I would do this deed or perish at the hands of Grendel. And to this I am bound; I will fulfill my oath and work the will of your people, or meet my death in this great hall.

Please note that excerpts and passages in the StudySync® library and this workbook are intended as touchstones to generate interest in an author's work. The excerpts and passages do not substitute for the reading of entire texts, and StudySync® strongly recommends that students seek out and purchase the whole literary or informational work in order to experience it as the author intended. Links to online resellers are available in our digital library. In addition, complete works may be ordered through an authorized reseller by filling out and returning to StudySync® the order form enclosed in this workbook.

Reading & Writing
Companion

13

Panel 8

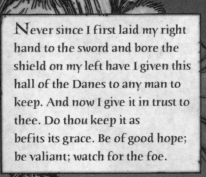

> Never since I first laid my right hand to the sword and bore the shield on my left have I given this hall of the Danes to any man to keep. And now I give it in trust to thee. Do thou keep it as befits its grace. Be of good hope; be valiant; watch for the foe.

Panel 9

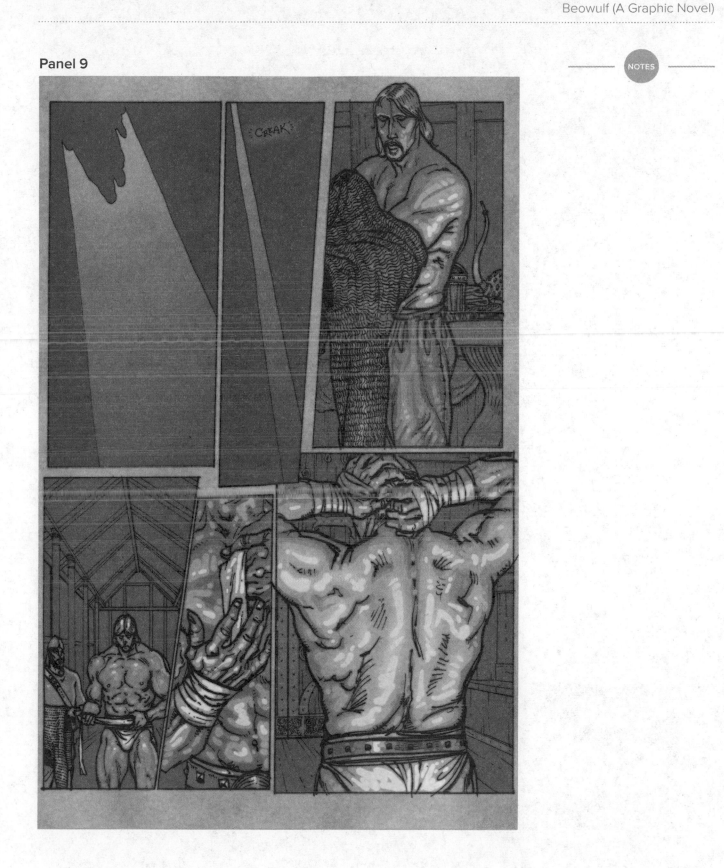

Panel 10

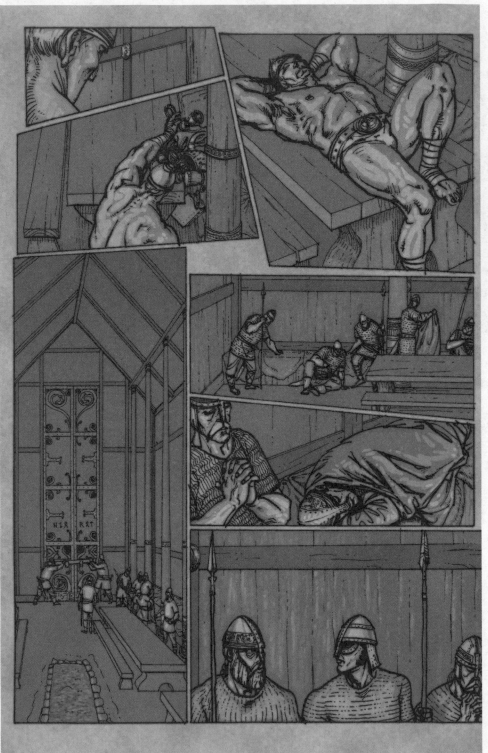

Panel 11

Panel 12

Panel 13

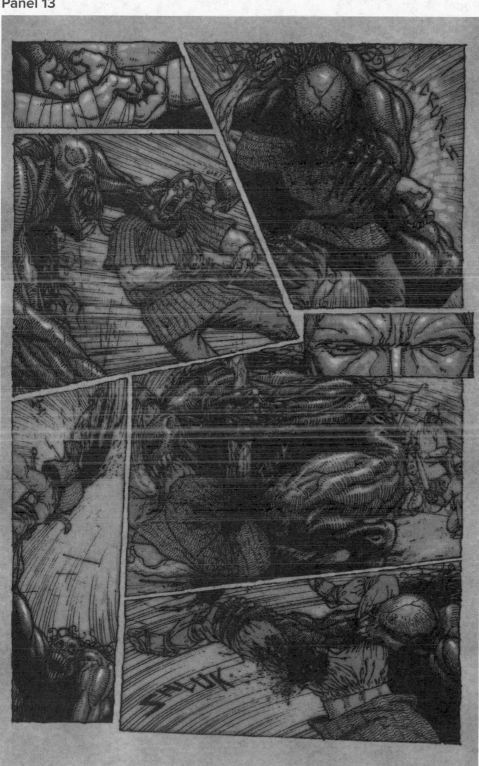

Panel 14

Panel 15

Please note that excerpts and passages in the StudySync® library and this workbook are intended as touchstones to generate interest in an author's work. The excerpts and passages do not substitute for the reading of entire texts, and StudySync® strongly recommends that students seek out and purchase the whole literary or informational work in order to experience it as the author intended. Links to online resellers are available in our digital library. In addition, complete works may be ordered through an authorized reseller by filling out and returning to StudySync® the order form enclosed in this workbook.

Reading & Writing Companion

21

Panel 16

Panel 17

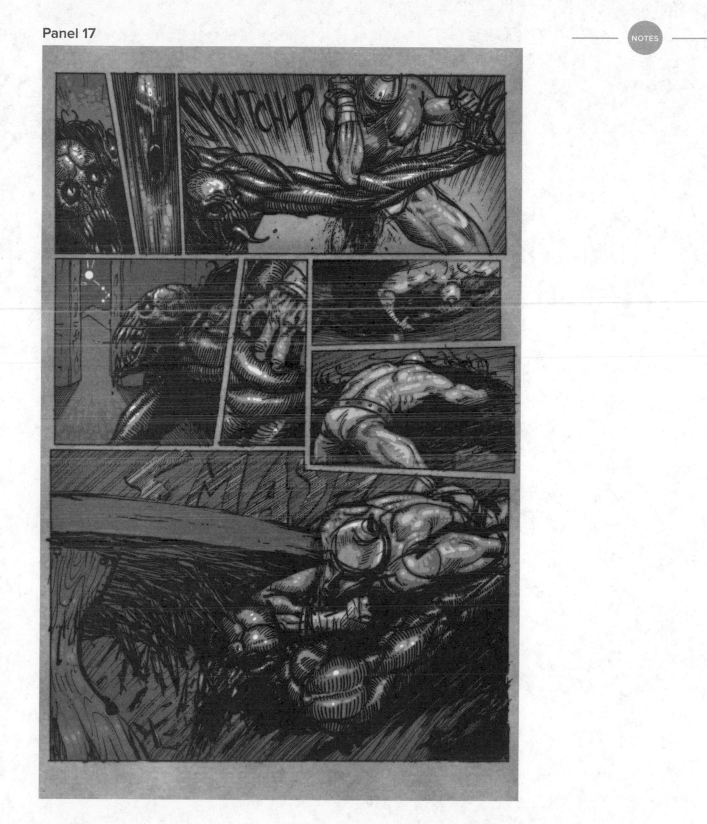

Please note that excerpts and passages in the StudySync® library and this workbook are intended as touchstones to generate interest in an author's work. The excerpts and passages do not substitute for the reading of entire texts, and StudySync® strongly recommends that students seek out and purchase the whole literary or informational work in order to experience it as the author intended. Links to online resellers are available in our digital library. In addition, complete works may be ordered through an authorized reseller by filling out and returning to StudySync® the order form enclosed in this workbook.

Reading & Writing Companion   23

Panel 18

Panel 19

Panel 20

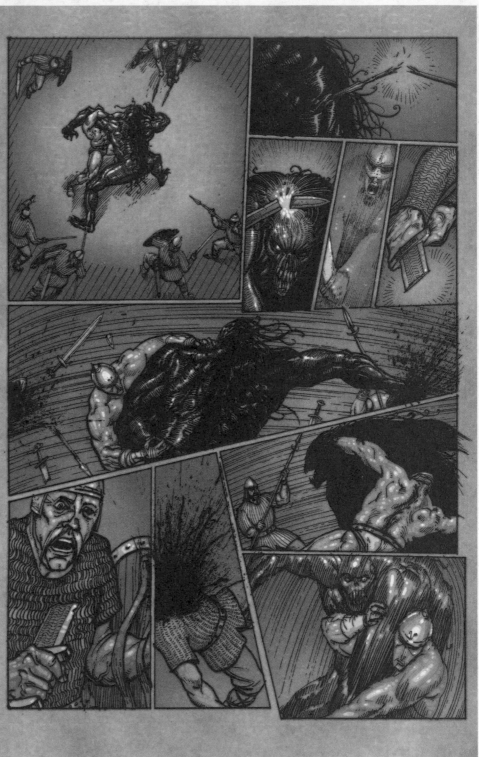

Panel 21

Please note that excerpts and passages in the StudySync® library and this workbook are intended as touchstones to generate interest in an author's work. The excerpts and passages do not substitute for the reading of entire texts, and StudySync® strongly recommends that students seek out and purchase the whole literary or informational work in order to experience it as the author intended. Links to online resellers are available in our digital library. In addition, complete works may be ordered through an authorized reseller by filling out and returning to StudySync® the order form enclosed in this workbook.

Reading & Writing Companion

27

Panel 22

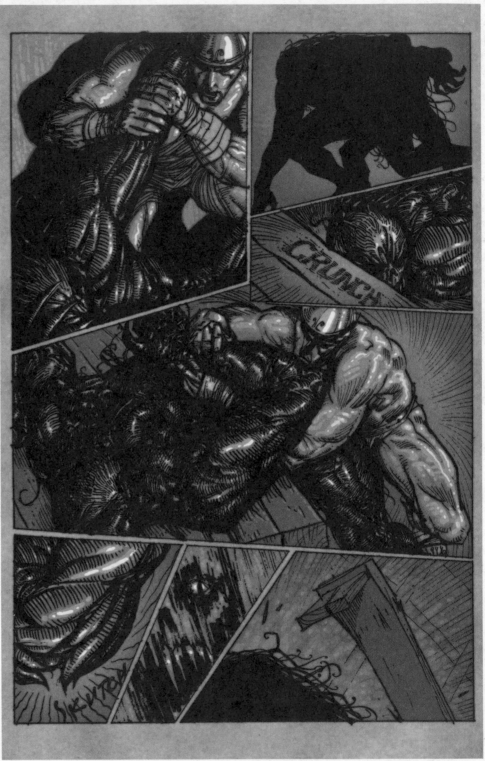

Panel 23

Panel 24

Reading & Writing Companion

Panel 25

Panel 26

Panel 27

Panel 28

Panel 29

Panel 30

BEOWULF. Copyright © 1999, 2000, 2007 by Gareth Hinds. Reproduced by permission of the publisher, Candlewick Press, Somerville, MA.

✏ WRITE

LITERARY ANALYSIS: How does the portrayal of Beowulf in this excerpt reveal the qualities of an Anglo-Saxon hero? Write a response in which you answer this question. Be sure to use textual evidence to defend your analysis of *Beowulf*.

Beowulf
(Lines 144–300)

POETRY
Anglo-Saxon Tradition
(translated by Seamus Heaney)
8th to 11th Centuries

Introduction

A foundational work of Old English literature dating from sometime between the 8th and 11th centuries, *Beowulf* narrates the deeds of a young nobleman from Geatland who comes to rid his Danish neighbors of a marauding monster, Grendel. In this modern translation of the epic poem, readers are introduced to Grendel's twelve-year reign of terror—and to the hero intent on stopping it—courtesy of poet and translator Seamus Heaney (1939–2013), the winner of the 1995 Nobel Prize in Literature. American poet Robert Lowell dubbed Heaney "the most important Irish poet since Yeats."

"No counsellor could ever expect fair reparation from those rabid hands."

144 So Grendel ruled in defiance of right,
145 one against all, until the greatest house
146 in the world stood empty, a deserted wallstead.
147 For twelve winters, seasons of woe,
148 the lord of the Shieldings[1] suffered under
149 his load of sorrow; and so, before long,
150 the news was known over the whole world.
151 Sad lays were sung about the beset king,
152 the vicious raids and ravages of Grendel,
153 his long and unrelenting feud,
154 nothing but war; how he would never
155 parley or make peace with any Dane
156 nor stop his death-dealing nor pay the death-price.
157 No counsellor could ever expect
158 fair **reparation** from those rabid hands.
159 All were endangered; young and old
160 were hunted down by that dark death-shadow
161 who lurked and swooped in the long nights
162 on the misty moors; nobody knows
163 where these reavers from hell roam on their errands.

164 So Grendel waged his lonely war,
165 inflicting constant cruelties on the people,
166 atrocious hurt. He took over Heorot[2],
167 haunted the glittering hall after dark,
168 but the throne itself, the treasure-seat,
169 he was kept from approaching; he was the Lord's outcast.

170 These were hard times, heart-breaking
171 for the prince of the Shieldings; powerful counsellors,
172 the highest in the land, would lend advice,

---

1. **Shieldings** descendants of a legendary royal family of Danes
2. **Heorot** represents the seat of Hrothgar's power, a mead-hall that is also a residence for the king's warriors

NOTES

Skill:
Word Patterns and
Relationships

The word lays *looks like a plural noun, since it comes after the adjective* sad *and before the verb* were. *Also, I suspect that* lays *are like songs, since the poem says they are "sung." I can try swapping* lays *for* songs . . .

Please note that excerpts and passages in the StudySync® library and this workbook are intended as touchstones to generate interest in an author's work. The excerpts and passages do not substitute for the reading of entire texts, and StudySync® strongly recommends that students seek out and purchase the whole literary or informational work in order to experience it as the author intended. Links to online resellers are available in our digital library. In addition, complete works may be ordered through an authorized reseller by filling out and returning to StudySync® the order form enclosed in this workbook.

Reading & Writing Companion 39

NOTES

173 plotting how best the bold defenders
174 might resist and beat off sudden attacks.
175 Sometimes at pagan shrines they vowed
176 offerings to idols, swore oaths
177 that the killer of souls might come to their aid
178 and save the people. That was their way,
179 their heathenish hope; deep in their hearts
180 they remembered hell. The Almighty Judge
181 of good deeds and bad, the Lord God,
182 Head of the Heavens and High King of the World,
183 was unknown to them. Oh, cursed is he
184 who in time of trouble has to thrust his soul
185 in the fire's embrace, **forfeiting** help;
186 he has nowhere to turn. But blessed is he
187 who after death can approach the Lord
188 and find friendship in the Father's embrace.

189 So that troubled time continued, woe
190 that never stopped, steady **affliction**
191 for Halfdane's son[3], too hard an ordeal.
192 There was panic after dark, people endured
193 raids in the night, riven by the terror.

194 When he heard about Grendel, Hygelac's thane[4]
195 was on home ground, over in Geatland.
196 There was no one else like him alive.
197 In his day, he was the mightiest man on earth,
198 high-born and powerful. He ordered a boat
199 that would ply the waves. He announced his plan:
200 to sail the swan's road and search out that king,
201 the famous prince who needed defenders.
202 Nobody tried to keep him from going,
203 no elder denied him, dear as he was to them.
204 Instead, they inspected omens and spurred
205 his ambition to go, whilst he moved about
206 like the leader he was, enlisting men,
207 the best he could find; with fourteen others
208 the warrior boarded the boat as captain,
209 a canny pilot along coast and currents.

210 Time went by, the boat was on water,
211 in close under the cliffs.

Skill:
Media

Heaney's translation sounds very different from the Old English and the Gummere translation: they sound more like a song. There is a little less alliteration in Heaney's translation. But this translation sounds more contemporary.

---

3. **Halfdane's son** King Hrothgar
4. **Hygelac's thane** a noble who provided military assistance to the King of the Geats, Hygelac

212 Men climbed eagerly up the gangplank,

213 sand churned in surf, warriors loaded

214 a cargo of weapons, shining war-gear

215 in the vessel's hold, then heaved out,

216 away with a will in their wood-wreathed ship.

217 Over the waves, with the wind behind her

218 and foam at her neck, she flew like a bird

219 until her curved prow had covered the distance

220 and on the following day, at the due hour,

221 those seafarers sighted land,

222 sunlit cliffs, sheer crags

223 and looming headlands, the landfall they sought.

224 It was the end of their voyage and the Geats vaulted

225 over the side, out on to the sand,

226 and moored their ship. There was a clash of mail

227 and a thresh of gear. They thanked God

228 for that easy crossing on a calm sea.

229 When the watchman on the wall, the Shieldings' lookout

230 whose job it was to guard the sea-cliffs,

231 saw shields glittering on the gangplank

232 and battle-equipment being unloaded

233 he had to find out who and what

234 the arrivals were. So he rode to the shore,

235 this horseman of Hrothgar's, and challenged them

236 in formal terms, **flourishing** his spear:

237 "What kind of men are you who arrive

238 rigged out for combat in coats of mail,

239 sailing here over the sea-lanes

240 in your steep-hulled boat? I have been stationed

241 as lookout on this coast for a long time.

242 My job is to watch the waves for raiders,

243 any danger to the Danish shore.

244 Never before has a force under arms

245 **disembarked** so openly—not bothering to ask

246 if the sentries allowed them safe passage

247 or the clan had consented. Nor have I seen

248 a mightier man-at-arms on this earth

249 than the one standing here: unless I am mistaken,

250 he is truly noble. This is no mere

251 hanger-on in a hero's armour.

252 So now, before you fare inland

253 as **interlopers**, I have to be informed

254 about who you are and where you hail from.

Please note that excerpts and passages in the StudySync® library and this workbook are intended as touchstones to generate interest in an author's work. The excerpts and passages do not substitute for the reading of entire texts, and StudySync® strongly recommends that students seek out and purchase the whole literary or informational work in order to experience it as the author intended. Links to online resellers are available in our digital library. In addition, complete works may be ordered through an authorized reseller by filling out and returning to StudySync® the order form enclosed in this workbook.

Reading & Writing Companion

41

NOTES

255   Outsiders from across the water,

256   I say it again: the sooner you tell

257   where you come from and why, the better."

258   The leader of the troop unlocked his word-hoard;

259   the distinguished one delivered this answer:

260   "We belong by birth to the Geat people

261   and owe allegiance to Lord Hygelac[5].

262   In his day, my father was a famous man,

263   a noble warrior-lord named Ecgtheow.

264   He outlasted many a long winter

265   and went on his way. All over the world

266   men wise in counsel continue to remember him.

267   We come in good faith to find your lord

268   and nation's shield, the son of Halfdane.

269   Give us the right advice and direction.

270   We have arrived here on a great errand

271   to the lord of the Danes, and I believe therefore

272   there should be nothing hidden or withheld between us.

273   So tell us if what we have heard is true

274   about this threat, whatever it is,

275   this danger abroad in the dark nights,

276   this corpse-maker mongering death

277   in the Shieldings' country. I come to proffer

278   my wholehearted help and counsel.

279   I can show the wise Hrothgar a way

280   to defeat his enemy and find respite—

281   if any respite is to reach him, ever.

282   I can calm the turmoil and terror in his mind.

283   Otherwise, he must endure woes

284   and live with grief for as long as his hall

285   stands at the horizon, on its high ground."

286   Undaunted, sitting astride his horse,

287   the coast-guard answered, "Anyone with gumption

288   and a sharp mind will take the measure

289   of two things: what's said and what's done.

290   I believe what you have told me: that you are a troop

291   loyal to our king. So come ahead

292   with your arms and your gear, and I will guide you.

293   What's more, I'll order my own comrades

294   on their word of honour to watch your boat

295   down there on the strand—keep her safe

---

5. **Lord Hygelac** King of the Geats and Beowulf's uncle

Reading & Writing Companion

296   in her fresh tar, until the time comes
297   for her curved prow to preen on the waves
298   and bear this hero back to Geatland.
299   May one so valiant and venturesome
300   come unharmed through the clash of battle."

Excerpted from *Beowulf: A New Verse Translation* by Seamus Heaney, published by W.W. Norton & Company.

First Read

Read *Beowulf*. After you read, complete the Think Questions below.

1. What violence did Grendel inflict on the Danes? Use specific details from the text to support your answer.

2. How do the Shieldings attempt to protect themselves? How effective are these means of protection? Be sure to cite textual evidence.

3. What is the coast-guard's initial opinion of the Geatland sailors? How does he react to their sudden arrival? Use evidence from the text to justify your answer.

4. Use context to determine the meaning of **affliction** as it is used in the text. Write your definition of *affliction* here and explain which context clues helped you determine its meaning.

5. Use context to determine the meaning of the noun **interloper** as it is used in the text. Write your definition of *interloper* here and explain which context clues helped you determine its meaning.

Skill:
Media

Use the Checklist to analyze Media in *Beowulf*. Refer to the sample student annotations about Media in the text.

••• CHECKLIST FOR MEDIA

In order to identify multiple interpretations of a story, drama, or poem, do the following:

- ✓ evaluate how each version interprets the source text

- ✓ consider how, within the same medium, a story can have multiple interpretations if told by writers from different time periods and cultures

- ✓ consider how stories told in the same medium will likely reflect the specific objectives as well as the respective ideas, concerns, and values of each writer

- ✓ note how the same information can be presented in more than one medium

- ✓ use the diverse media to cross-check information

- ✓ consider the skillfulness and artistry of various translations of the same text

To analyze multiple interpretations of a story, drama, or poem, evaluating how each version interprets the source text, consider the following questions:

- ✓ What medium is being used, and how does it affect the interpretation of the source text?

- ✓ What are the similarities and differences between the various versions?

- ✓ If each version is from a different time period/culture, what does each version reveal about the author's objectives, time period and culture in which it was written?

- ✓ How can you integrate multiple sources presented in diverse formats and media in order to inform your own interpretation of the story?

Skill:
Media

To analyze different versions of Beowulf, read an excerpt from the Old English following along with the video, then compare the Gummere equivalent. Next, reread a section from the Heaney translation. Then, using the checklist on the previous page, answer the multiple-choice questions that follow.

⟳ YOUR TURN

From *Beowulf* (Old English version)

Syððan ærest wearð
feasceaft funden, he þæs frofre gebad,
weox under wolcnum, weorðmyndum þah,
oðþæt him æghwylc þara ymbsittendra
ofer hronrade hyran scolde,
gomban gyldan. þæt wæs god cyning.

From *Beowulf,* translated by Francis B. Gummere

Since erst he lay
friendless, a foundling, fate repaid him:
for he waxed under welkin, in wealth he throve,
till before him the folk, both far and near,
who house by the whale-path, heard his
mandate, gave him gifts: a good king he!

From *Beowulf,* (translated by Seamus Heaney)
Note: *These lines are from another section of the poem.*

So Grendel ruled in defiance of right,
one against all, until the greatest house
in the world stood empty, a deserted wallstead.
For twelve winters, seasons of woe,
the lord of the Shieldings suffered under
his load of sorrow; and so, before long,
the news was known over the whole world.
Sad lays were sung about the beset king,
the vicious raids and ravages of Grendel,
his long and unrelenting feud,
nothing but war; how he would never
parley or make peace with any Dane
nor stop his death-dealing nor pay the
death-price.
No counsellor could ever expect
fair reparation from those rabid hands.
All were endangered; young and old
were hunted down by that dark death-shadow
who lurked and swooped in the long nights
on the misty moors; nobody knows
where these reavers from hell roam on their
errands.

1. When watching and listening to the Old English being recited in the video, and reading the same lines in the Gummere translation, how is the translation similar to the original poem?

   ○ A. Gummere attempted to keep the vowel patterns of the original poem the same.
   ○ B. Gummere attempted to use mostly archaic words.
   ○ C. Gummere attempted to keep the alliterative patterns of the original poem the same.
   ○ D. Gummere attempted to make the poem rhyme.

2. When comparing the Old English version to the Heaney translation, how is it different?

   ○ A. Heaney uses conjoined words to keep his text more compact.
   ○ B. Heaney uses fewer archaic words, making his translation more contemporary.
   ○ C. Heaney's version is shorter and more concise
   ○ D. All of the above

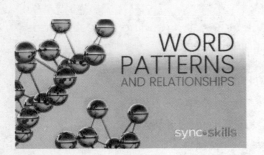

Skill:
Word Patterns and Relationships

Use the Checklist to analyze Word Patterns and Relationships in *Beowulf*. Refer to the sample student annotations about Word Patterns and Relationships in the text.

••• CHECKLIST FOR WORD PATTERNS AND RELATIONSHIPS

In order to identify patterns of word changes to indicate different meanings or parts of speech, do the following:

- ✓ determine the word's part of speech

- ✓ when reading, use context clues to make a preliminary determination of the meaning of the word

- ✓ when writing a response to a text, check that you understand the meaning and part of speech and that it makes sense in your sentence

- ✓ consult a dictionary to verify your preliminary determination of the meanings and parts of speech

- ✓ be sure to read all of the definitions, and then decide which definition, form, and part of speech makes sense within the context of the text

To identify and correctly use patterns of word changes that indicate different meanings or parts of speech, consider the following questions:

- ✓ What is the intended meaning of the word?

- ✓ How do I know that this word form is the correct part of speech? Do I understand the word patterns for this particular word?

- ✓ When I consult a dictionary, can I confirm that the meaning I have determined for this word is correct? Do I know how to use it correctly?

Skill:
Word Patterns and Relationships

Reread the fourth stanza from *Beowulf*. Then, using the Checklist on the previous page, answer the multiple-choice questions below.

⟳ YOUR TURN

1. What part of speech is the word *ordeal*?

   ○ A. noun
   ○ B. verb
   ○ C. adjective
   ○ D. adverb

2. Paying close attention to parts of speech and context, determine which of the following words most closely means *distressed*.

   ○ A. woe
   ○ B. endured
   ○ C. riven
   ○ D. ordeal

Close Read

Reread *Beowulf*. As you reread, complete the Skills Focus questions below. Then use your answers and annotations from the questions to help you complete the Write activity.

◎ SKILLS FOCUS

1. *Beowulf* is an Old English poem that contains many words related to the English words we use today. Translators like Seamus Heaney often choose to keep some of these words, even if they are archaic or not familiar to us. Find two examples of these words in the Heaney translation and use your knowledge of Word Patterns and Relationships to determine their part of speech, and use contextual clues to help you guess a meaning.

2. In Seamus Heaney's translation, Beowulf spends time building up a force of fourteen heavily armed men before traveling to the hall to challenge Grendel. Identify a difference in the way Beowulf's quest is portrayed in the graphic novel, and explain how that difference changes your perception of the character.

3. Find details that show how the historical and social setting of *Beowulf* affects the way Beowulf and other characters interact. Explain which historical and social details you think are particularly effective in developing this part of the plot and why.

4. In the opening lines of this Heaney excerpt, we find out that "These were hard times, heart-breaking for the prince of the Shieldings." It is upon hearing this news that Beowulf decides to travel to the Shieldings and help them. How do these times of challenge reveal the true values of an Anglo-Saxon hero? Highlight and annotate two pieces of textual evidence to support your answer.

✎ WRITE

DISCUSSION: The two excerpts (the Heaney translation and the Hinds graphic novel) of *Beowulf* demonstrate a universal pattern in literature. People are living in fear as an evil force threatens to upset society. Then a brave, strong, and good hero appears to defeat the evil force. What would a hero's arrival look like in a modern-day setting? What would the application of Anglo-Saxon values look like in today's society and culture? Discuss this question with a group of your peers. To prepare for your discussion, use the graphic organizer to write down your ideas about the prompt. Support your ideas with evidence from the text. After your discussion, you will write a reflection in the space below.

Sir Gawain and the Green Knight

POETRY
Anonymous
14th Century
(translated by Simon Armitage)

Introduction

Sir Gawain and the Green Knight is a 14th-century Arthurian romance that has been retold by myriad storytellers since. Originally written in alliterative verse by an unknown author, this translation, in free verse, was published in 2008 by English poet Simon Armitage (b. 1963), an award-winning writer and lecturer from Yorkshire who is most famous for his darkly comedic poetry, drama, and prose. With themes of courage and competition, Sir Gawain and the Green Knight weaves together two traditional motifs: the beheading game, and the exchange of winnings. In this particular excerpt, a mysterious visitor arrives during a holiday feast and issues a daunting challenge.

"Amazement seized their minds, no soul had ever seen a knight of such a kind—"

NOTES

1 Flavorsome **delicacies** of flesh were fetched in
2 and the freshest of foods, so many in fact
3 there was scarcely space to present the stews
4 or to set the soups in the silver bowls on
5 the cloth.
6 Each guest received his share
7 of bread or meat or broth;
8 a dozen plates per pair—
9 plus beer or wine, or both!

10 Now, on the subject of supper I'll say no more
11 as it's obvious to everyone that no one went without.
12 Because another sound, a new sound, suddenly drew near,
13 which might signal the king to sample his supper,
14 for barely had the horns finished blowing their breath
15 and with starters just spooned to the seated guests,
16 a fearful form appeared, framed in the door:
17 a mountain of a man, immeasurably high,
18 a hulk of a human from head to hips,
19 so long and thick in his loins and his limbs
20 I should genuinely judge him to be a half giant,
21 or a most massive man, the mightiest of mortals.
22 But handsome, too, like any horseman worth his horse,
23 for despite the bulk and brawn of his body
24 his stomach and waist were slender and sleek.
25 In fact in all features he was finely formed
26 it seemed.
27 Amazement seized their minds,
28 no soul had ever seen
29 a knight of such a kind—
30 entirely emerald green.

31 And his gear and garments were green as well:
32 a tight fitting tunic, tailored to his torso,
33 and a cloak to cover him, the cloth fully lined

NOTES

34 with smoothly shorn fur clearly showing, and faced
35 with all-white ermine, as was the hood,
36 worn shawled on his shoulders, shucked from his head.
37 On his lower limbs his leggings were also green,
38 wrapped closely round his calves, and his sparkling spurs
39 were green-gold, strapped with stripy silk,
40 and were set on his stockings, for this stranger was shoeless.
41 In all vestments he revealed himself veritably verdant!
42 From his belt hooks and buckle to the baubles and gems
43 arrayed so richly around his costume
44 and adorning the saddle, stitched onto silk.
45 All the details of his dress are difficult to describe,
46 embroidered as it was with butterflies and birds,
47 green beads emblazoned on a background of gold.
48 All the horse's tack—harness strap, hind strap,
49 the eye of the bit, each alloy and enamel
50 and the stirrups he stood in were similarly tinted,
51 and the same with the cantle and the skirts of the saddle,
52 all glimmering and glinting with the greenest jewels.
53 And the horse: every hair was green, from hoof
54 to mane.
55 A steed of pure green stock.
56 Each snort and shudder strained
57 the hand-stitched bridle, but
58 his rider had him reined.

59 The fellow in green was in fine fettle.
60 The hair of his head was as green as his horse,
61 fine flowing locks which fanned across his back,
62 plus a bushy green beard growing down to his breast,
63 and his face hair along with the hair of his head
64 was lopped in a line at elbow length
65 so half his arms were gowned in green growth,
66 crimped at the collar, like a king's cape.
67 The mane of his mount was groomed to match,
68 combed and knotted into curlicues
69 then tinseled with gold, tied and twisted
70 green over gold, green over gold. . . .
71 The fetlocks were finished in the same fashion
72 with bright green ribbon braided with beads,
73 as was the tail—to its tippety-tip!
74 And a long, tied thong lacing it tight
75 was strung with gold bells which resounded and shone.
76 No waking man had witnessed such a warrior
77 or weird warhorse—otherworldly, yet flesh

78 and bone.

79 A look of lightning flashed

80 from somewhere in his soul.

81 The force of that man's fist

82 would be a thunderbolt.

83 Yet he wore no helmet and no hauberk either,

84 no armored apparel or plate was apparent,

85 and he swung no sword nor sported any shield,

86 but held in one hand a sprig of holly—

87 of all the evergreens the greenest ever—

88 and in the other hand held the mother of all axes,

89 a cruel piece of kit I kid you not:

90 the head was an ell in length at least

91 and forged in green steel with a gilt finish;

92 the skull-busting blade was so stropped and buffed

93 it could shear a man's scalp and shave him to boot.

94 The handle which fitted that fiend's great fist

95 was inlaid with iron, end to end,

96 with green pigment picking out impressive designs.

97 From stock to neck, where it stopped with a knot,

98 a lace was looped the length of the haft,

99 trimmed with tassels and tails of string

100 fastened firmly in place by forest-green buttons.

101 And he kicks on, canters through that crowded hall

102 towards the top table, not the least bit timid,

103 cocksure of himself, sitting high in the saddle.

104 "And who," he bellows, without breaking breath,

105 "is governor of this gaggle? I'll be glad to know.

106 It's with him and him alone that I'll have

107 my say."

108 The green man steered his gaze

109 deep into every eye,

110 explored each person's face

111 to probe for a reply.

112 The guests looked on. They gaped and they gawked

113 and were mute with amazement: what did it mean

114 that human and horse could develop this hue,

115 should grow to be grass-green or greener still,

116 like green enamel emboldened by bright gold?

117 Some stood and stared then stepped a little closer,

118 drawn near to the knight to know his next move;

119 they'd seen some sights, but this was something special,

120 a miracle or magic, or so they imagined.

121 Yet several of the lords were like statues in their seats,

122 left speechless and rigid, not risking a response.

123 The hall fell hushed, as if all who were present

124 had slipped into sleep or some trancelike state.

125 No doubt

126 not all were stunned and stilled

127 by dread, but duty bound

128 to hold their tongues

129 until their **sovereign** could respond.

130 Then the king acknowledged this curious occurrence,

131 cordially addressed him, keeping his cool.

132 "A warm welcome, sir, this winter's night.

133 My name is Arthur, I am head of this house.

134 Won't you slide from that saddle and stay awhile,

135 and the business which brings you we shall learn of later."

136 "No," said the knight, "it's not in my nature

137 to idle or dally about this evening.

138 But because your acclaim is so loudly chorused,

139 and your castle and brotherhood are called the best,

140 the strongest men to ever mount the saddle,

141 the worthiest knights ever known to the world,

142 both in competition and true combat,

143 and since courtesy, so it's said, is championed here,

144 I'm intrigued, and attracted to your door at this time.

145 Be assured by this hollin stem here in my hand

146 that I mean no menace. So expect no **malice**,

147 for if I'd slogged here tonight to slay and slaughter

148 my helmet and hauberk wouldn't be at home

149 and my sword and spear would be here at my side,

150 and more weapons of war, as I'm sure you're aware;

151 I'm clothed for peace, not kitted out for conflict.

152 But if you're half as honorable as I've heard folk say

153 you'll gracefully grant me this game which I ask for

154 by right."

155 Then Arthur answered, "Knight

156 most **courteous**, you claim

157 a fair, unarmored fight.

158 We'll see you have the same."

159 "I'm spoiling for no scrap, I swear. Besides,

160 the bodies on these benches are just bum-fluffed bairns.

161 If I'd ridden to your castle rigged out for a ruck[1]

---

1. **rigged out for a ruck** prepared for a fight

162 these lightweight adolescents wouldn't last a minute.

163 But it's Yuletide—a time of youthfulness, yes?

164 So at Christmas in this court I lay down a challenge:

165 if a person here present, within these premises,

166 is big or bold or red blooded enough

167 to strike me one stroke and be struck in return,

168 I shall give him as a gift this gigantic cleaver

169 and the axe shall be his to handle how he likes.

170 I'll kneel, bare my neck and take the first knock.

171 So who has the gall? The gumption? The guts?

172 Who'll spring from his seat and snatch this weapon?

173 I offer the axe—who'll have it as his own?

174 I'll afford one free hit from which I won't flinch,

175 and promise that twelve months will pass in peace,

176 then claim

177 the duty I deserve

178 in one year and one day.

179 Does no one have the nerve

180 to wager in this way?"

181 Flustered at first, now totally foxed

182 were the household and the lords, both the highborn and the low.

183 Still stirruped, the knight swiveled round in his saddle

184 looking left and right, his red eyes rolling

185 beneath the bristles of his bushy green brows,

186 his beard swishing from side to side.

187 When the court kept its counsel he cleared his throat

188 and stiffened his spine. Then he spoke his mind:

189 "So here is the House of Arthur," he scoffed,

190 "whose virtues reverberate across vast realms.

191 Where's the **fortitude** and fearlessness you're so famous for?

192 And the breathtaking bravery and the big-mouth bragging?

193 The towering reputation of the Round Table,

194 skittled and scuppered by a stranger—what a scandal!

195 You flap and you flinch and I've not raised a finger!"

196 Then he laughed so loud that their leader saw red.

197 Blood flowed to his fine-featured face and he raged

198 inside.

199 His men were also hurt—

200 those words had pricked their pride.

201 But born so brave at heart

202 the king stepped up one stride.

203 "Your request," he countered, "is quite insane,

204 and folly finds the man who flirts with the fool.

205   No warrior worth his salt would be worried by your words,

206   so in heaven's good name hand over the axe

207   and I'll happily fulfill the favor you ask."

208   He strides to him swiftly and seizes his arm;

209   the man-mountain dismounts in one mighty leap.

210   Then Arthur grips the axe, grabs it by its haft

211   and takes it above him, intending to attack.

212   Yet the stranger before him stands up straight,

213   highest in the house by at least a head.

214   Quite simply he stands there stroking his beard,

215   fiddling with his coat, his face without fear,

216   about to be bludgeoned, but no more bothered

217   than a guest at the table being given a goblet

218   of wine.

219   By Guinevere, Gawain

220   now to his king inclines

221   and says, "I stake my claim.

222   This moment must be mine."

223   "Should you call me, courteous lord," said Gawain to his king,

224   "to rise from my seat and stand at your side,

225   politely take leave of my place at the table

226   and quit without causing offence to my queen,

227   then I shall come to your counsel before this great court.

228   For I find it unfitting, as my fellow knights would,

229   when a deed of such daring is dangled before us

230   that you take on this trial—tempted as you are—

231   when brave, bold men are seated on these benches,

232   men never matched in the mettle of their minds,

233   never beaten or bettered in the field of battle.

234   I am weakest of your warriors and feeblest of wit;

235   loss of my life would be grieved the least.

236   Were I not your nephew my life would mean nothing;

237   To be born of our blood is my body's only claim.

238   Such a foolish affair is unfitting for a king,

239   so, being first to come forward, it should fall to me.

240   And if my proposal is improper, let no other person

241   stand blame."

242   The knighthood then unites

243   and each knight says the same:

244   their king can stand aside

245   and give Gawain the game.

246   So the sovereign instructed his knight to stand.

247   Getting to his feet he moved graciously forward

NOTES

248   and knelt before Arthur, taking hold of the axe.

249   Letting go of it, Arthur then held up his hand

250   to give young Gawain the blessing of God

251   and hope he finds firmness in heart and fist.

252   "Take care, young cousin, to catch him cleanly,

253   use full-blooded force then you needn't fear

254   the blow which he threatens to trade in return."

255   Gawain, with the weapon, walked towards the warrior,

256   and they stood face-to-face, not one man afraid.

257   Then the green knight spoke, growled at Gawain:

258   "Before we compete, repeat what we've promised.

259   And start by saying your name to me, sir,

260   and tell me the truth so I can take it on trust."

261   "In good faith, it's Gawain," said the God-fearing knight,

262   "I heave this axe, and whatever happens after,

263   in twelvemonth's time I'll be struck in return

264   with any weapon you wish, and by you and you

265   alone."

266   The other answers, says

267   "Well, by my living bones,

268   I welcome you Gawain

269   to bring the blade-head home."

270   "Gawain," said the green knight, "by God, I'm glad

271   the favor I've called for will fall from your fist.

272   You've perfectly repeated the promise we've made

273   and the terms of the contest are crystal clear.

274   Except for one thing: you must solemnly swear

275   that you'll seek me yourself; that you'll search me out

276   to the ends of the earth to earn the same blow

277   as you'll dole out today in this decorous hall."

278   "But where will you be? Where's your abode?

279   You're a man of mystery, as God is my maker.

280   Which court do you come from and what are you called?

281   There is knowledge I need, including your name,

282   then by wit I'll work out the way to your door

283   and keep to our contract, so cross my heart."

284   "But enough at New Year. It needs nothing more,"

285   said the war man in green to worthy Gawain.

286   "I could tell you the truth once you've taken the blow;

287   if you smite me smartly I could spell out the facts

288   of my house and home and my name, if it helps,

289   Then you'll pay me a visit and vouch for our pact.

290   Or if I keep quiet you might cope much better,

291   loafing and lounging here, looking no further. But

292 you stall!
293 Now grasp that gruesome axe
294 And show your striking style."
295 He answered, "since you ask,"
296 And touched the tempered steel.

297 In the standing position he prepared to be struck,
298 bent forward, revealing a flash of green flesh
299 as he heaped his hair to the crown of his head,
300 the nape of his neck now naked and ready.
301 Gawain grips the axe and heaves it heavenwards
302 plants his left foot firmly on the floor in front,
303 then swings it swiftly towards the bare skin.
304 The cleanness of the strike cleaved the spinal cord
305 and parted the fat and the flesh so far
306 that the bright steel blade took a bite from the floor.
307 The handsome head tumbles onto the earth
308 and the king's men kick it as it clatters past.
309 Blood gutters brightly against his green gown,
310 yet the man doesn't shudder or stagger or sink
311 but trudges towards them on those tree-trunk legs
312 and rummages around, reaches at their feet
313 and cops hold of his head and hoists it high,
314 and strides to his steed, snatches the bridle,
315 steps into the stirrups and swings onto the saddle
316 still gripping his head by a handful of hair.
317 Then he settles himself in his seat with the ease
318 of a man unmarked, never mind being minus
319 his head!
320 And when he wheeled about
321 his bloody neck still bled.
322 His point was proved. The court
323 was deadened now with dread.

324 For that scalp and skull now swung from his fist;
325 towards the top table he turned the face
326 and it opened its eyelids, started straight ahead
327 and spoke this speech, which you'll hear for yourselves:
328 "Sir Gawain, be wise enough to keep your word
329 and faithfully follow me until I'm found
330 as you vowed in this hall within hearing of these horsemen.
331 You're charged with getting to the Green Chapel,
332 To reap what you've sown. You'll rightfully receive
333 the justice you are due just as January dawns.
334 Men know my name as the Green Chapel knight

NOTES

335   and even a fool couldn't fail to find me.

336   So come, or be called a coward forever."

337   With a tug of the reigns he twisted around

338   and, head still in hand, galloped out of the hall,

339   so the hooves brought the fire from the flame in the flint.

340   Which Kingdom he came from they hadn't a clue,

341   no more than they knew where he made for next.

342   And then?

343   Well, with the green man gone

344   they laughed and grinned again.

345   And yet such goings-on

346   were magic to those men.

347   And although King Arthur was awestruck at heart

348   No signed of it showed. Instead he spoke

349   to his queen of queens with courteous words:

350   "Dear lady, don't be daunted by this deed today,

351   it's in keeping that such strangeness should occur at Christmas

352   between sessions of banter and seasonal song,

353   amid the lively pastimes of ladies and lords.

354   And at the least I'm allowed to eat at last,

355   having witnessed such wonder, wouldn't you say?

356   Then he glanced at Gawain and was **graceful** with his words:

357   "Now hang up your axe—one hack is enough."

358   So it dangled from the drape behind the dais²

359   so that men who saw it would be mesmerised and amazed,

360   And give it voice, on its evidence, to the stunning event.

361   Then the two of them turned and walked to the table,

362   the monarch and his man, and were met with food—

363   double dishes apiece, rare delicacies,

364   all manners of meals—and the music of minstrels.

365   And they danced and sang till the sun went down

366   that day.

367   But mind your mood, Gawain,

368   keep blacker thoughts at bay,

369   or lose this lethal game

370   you've promised you will play.

From SIR GAWAIN AND THE GREEN KNIGHT: A NEW VERSE TRANSLATION, translated by Simon Armitage. Copyright © 2007 by Simon Armitage. Used by permission of W. W. Norton & Company, Inc.

---

2. **dais** a raised platform upon which sits a throne

✎ WRITE

LITERARY ANALYSIS: How does the portrayal of Gawain in this excerpt reveal the values and code of conduct of medieval knights? Use textual evidence and original commentary to support your response.

Truth Serum

POETRY
Naomi Shihab Nye
2005

Introduction

Naomi Shihab Nye (b. 1952) is an American poet living in San Antonio, Texas. Raised in both Jerusalem and San Antonio, Nye often focuses on ancestry and cultural differences in her writing, celebrating the everyday occurrences of life. She is considered one of the great poets of the American Southwest and has published many critically acclaimed volumes of poetry. "Truth Serum" was included in Nye's 2005 collection *You & Yours*.

"That frog song wanting nothing but echo? / We used that."

1   We made it from the ground-up corn in the old back **pasture**.
2   Pinched a scent of night jasmine **billowing** off the fence,
3   popped it right in.
4   That frog song wanting nothing but echo?
5   We used that.
6   Stirred it widely. Noticed the clouds while stirring.
7   Called upon our **ancient** great aunts and their long slow eyes
8   of summer. Dropped in their names.
9   Added a mint leaf now and then
10 to hearten the broth. Added a note of cheer and worry.
11 Orange butterfly between the claps of thunder?
12 Perfect. And once we had it,
13 had smelled and tasted the **fragrant** syrup,
14 placing the pan on a back burner for keeping,
15 the sorrow lifted in small ways.
16 We boiled down the lies in another pan till they disappeared.
17 We washed that pan.

Naomi Shihab Nye, "Truth Serum" from You & Yours. Copyright © 2005 by Naomi Shihab Nye. Reprinted with the permission of The Permissions Company, Inc. on behalf of BOA Editions, Ltd., www.boaeditions.org.

✏ WRITE

POETRY: Think about places, people, and experiences that bring truth and happiness into your life. Then write a poem about "Truth Serum" as you see it applied to your life. You may use Naomi Shihab Nye's poem, including her use of sensory details, as a model for your own writing.

Please note that excerpts and passages in the StudySync® library and this workbook are intended as touchstones to generate interest in an author's work. The excerpts and passages do not substitute for the reading of entire texts, and StudySync® strongly recommends that students seek out and purchase the whole literary or informational work in order to experience it as the author intended. Links to online resellers are available in our digital library. In addition, complete works may be ordered through an authorized reseller by filling out and returning to StudySync® the order form enclosed in this workbook.

Reading & Writing Companion   63

Richard III

DRAMA
William Shakespeare
1592

Introduction

n this famous soliloquy from the opening of Shakespeare's *Richard III*, Richard muses on his circumstances and his plans to seize the throne from his brother through murder, lies, and betrayal.

"Now is the winter of our discontent / Made glorious summer by this son of York."

From Act I, Scene i:

Characters:
RICHARD, DUKE OF GLOUCESTER: brother to the King Edward IV, afterwards King Richard III

Location: *London. A street.*

1 [*Enter* RICHARD DUKE of GLOUCESTER, *solus.*]

2 GLOUCESTER: Now is the winter of our discontent

3 Made glorious summer by this son of York[1];

4 And all the clouds that low'r'd upon our house

5 In the deep bosom of the ocean buried.

6 Now are our brows bound with victorious wreaths,

7 Our bruised arms hung up for monuments,

8 Our stern alarums[2] chang'd to merry meetings,

9 Our dreadful marches to delightful measures.

10 Grim-visag'd War hath smooth'd his wrinkled front;

11 And now, in stead of mounting barded steeds

12 To fright the souls of fearful adversaries,

13 He capers nimbly in a lady's chamber

14 To the **lascivious** pleasing of a lute.

15 But I, that am not shap'd for sportive tricks,

16 Nor made to court an amorous looking-glass;

17 I, that am rudely stamp'd, and **want** love's majesty

18 To strut before a **wanton** ambling nymph;

19 I, that am curtail'd of this fair proportion,

20 Cheated of feature by **dissembling** nature,

21 Deform'd, unfinish'd, sent before my time

22 Into this breathing world, scarce half made up,

Engraving of King Richard III, 1611

---

1. **son of York** Richard's brother, King Edward IV, of the York family
2. **stern alarums** alarms, or calls to battle

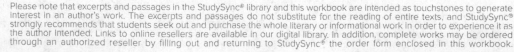

23 And that so lamely and unfashionable

24 That dogs bark at me as I halt by them—

25 Why, I, in this weak piping time of peace,

26 Have no delight to pass away the time,

27 Unless to see my shadow in the sun

28 And **descant** on mine own deformity.

29 And therefore, since I cannot prove a lover

30 To entertain these fair well-spoken days,

31 I am determined to prove a villain

32 And hate the idle pleasures of these days.

33 Plots have I laid, inductions dangerous,

34 By drunken prophecies, libels, and dreams,

35 To set my brother Clarence and the King

36 In deadly hate the one against the other;

37 And if King Edward be as true and just

38 As I am subtle, false, and treacherous,

39 This day should Clarence closely be mew'd up

40 About a prophecy, which says that G

41 Of Edward's heirs the murtherer shall be.

42 Dive, thoughts, down to my soul, here Clarence comes!

✏ WRITE

CORRESPONDENCE: In the persona of Richard III, write a confessional letter explaining why you choose to be a villain. Use your own words to paraphrase the reasons stated in the soliloquy, but maintain the meaning and logical order of the original text.

The Pardoner's Prologue
(from *The Canterbury Tales*)

POETRY
Geoffrey Chaucer
1387

Introduction

On a pilgrimage from London to Canterbury Cathedral to visit the shrine of St. Thomas Becket, twenty-nine people from various walks of life engage in a storytelling contest. Despite the fact that they are gathered for a spiritual purpose, many of them seem distracted by more earthly concerns. Their two dozen stories comprise *The Canterbury Tales* by Geoffrey Chaucer (c. 1343–1400), one of the foundational works of English literature. Offering social commentary that is not without humor, irony, and wit, the collection features classic musings like "The Pardoner's Prologue," in which the Pardoner—a sort of preacher who sells promises of salvation for a price—introduces himself to the group by launching into an irreverent confession about his professional behavior.

"When they are dead, for all I think thereon / Their souls may well black-berrying have gone!"

NOTES

Skill:
Point of View

The Pardoner is revealing something to the reader. This stanza suggests he is a performer and has his lines memorized. His audience probably thinks his sermon is honest and isn't aware it's a performance.

Skill:
Point of View

This reminds me of the beginning. The relics don't actually have power, but the audience doesn't share that knowledge. He is taking advantage of them and exaggerating the powers of the objects.

1 **from The Prologue of the Pardoner's Tale:**

2 "Masters," quoth he, "in churches, when I preach,
3 I am at pains that all shall hear my speech,
4 And ring it out as roundly as a bell,
5 For I know all by heart the thing I tell.
6 My **theme** is always one, and ever was:
7 '*Radix malorum est cupiditas*.[1]'

8 "First I announce the place whence I have come,
9 And then I show my pardons, all and some.
10 Our liege-lord's seal on my patent perfect,
11 I show that first, my safety to protect,
12 And then no man's so old, no priest nor clerk,
13 As to disturb me in Christ's holy work;
14 And after that my tales I marshal all.
15 Indulgences of pope and cardinal,
16 Of **patriarch** and bishop, these I do
17 Show, and in Latin speak some words, a few,
18 To spice therewith a bit my sermoning
19 And stir men to devotion, marvelling.
20 Then show I forth my hollow crystal-stones,
21 Which are crammed full of rags, aye, and of bones;
22 Relics are these, as they think, every one.
23 Then I've in latten box a shoulder bone
24 Which came out of a holy Hebrew's sheep.
25 'Good men,' say I, 'my words in memory keep;
26 If this bone shall be washed in any well,
27 Then if a cow, calf, sheep, or ox should swell
28 That's eaten snake, or been by serpent stung,
29 Take water of that well and wash its tongue,
30 And 'twill be well anon; and furthermore,
31 Of pox and scab and every other sore

---

1. **Radix malorum est cupiditas** translated from Biblical Latin: "the root of evil is greed"

NOTES

32 Shall every sheep be healed that of this well
33 Drinks but one draught; take heed of what I tell.
34 And if the man that owns the beasts, I trow,
35 Shall every week, and that before cock-crow,
36 And before breakfast, drink thereof a draught,
37 As that Jew taught of yore in his priestcraft,
38 His beasts and all his store shall multiply.
39 And, good sirs, it's a cure for jealousy;
40 For though a man be fallen in jealous rage,
41 Let one make of this water his pottage
42 And nevermore shall he his wife mistrust,
43 Though he may know the truth of all her lust,
44 Even though she'd taken two priests, aye, or three.

45 " 'Here is a mitten, too, that you may see.
46 Who puts his hand therein, I say again,
47 He shall have increased harvest of his grain,
48 After he's sown, be it of wheat or oats,
49 Just so he offers pence or offers groats.

50 " 'Good men and women, one thing I warn you,
51 If any man be here in church right now
52 That's done a sin so horrible that he
53 Dare not, for shame of that sin **shriven** be,
54 Or any woman, be she young or old,
55 That's made her husband into a cuckold[2],
56 Such folk shall have no power and no grace
57 To offer to my relics in this place.
58 But whoso finds himself without such blame,
59 He will come up and offer, in God's name,
60 And I'll absolve him by authority
61 That has, by bull, been granted unto me.'

62 "By this fraud have I won me, year by year,
63 A hundred marks, since I've been pardoner.
64 I stand up like a scholar in a pulpit,
65 And when the ignorant people all do sit,
66 I preach, as you have heard me say before,
67 And tell a hundred false japes, less or more.
68 I am at pains, then, to stretch forth my neck,
69 And east and west upon the folk I beck,
70 As does a dove that's sitting on a barn.
71 With hands and swift tongue, then, do I so yarn

2. **cuckold** has been sexually unfaithful to

Skill:
Connotation
and Denotation

I think the word "fraud" can have negative connotations. The Pardoner seems to admit he has a habit of lying to "ignorant people."

The dictionary definition of "fraud" is "wrongful or criminal deception" which confirms the negative connotation as it is used.

NOTES

72   That it's a joy to see my busyness.

73   Of **avarice** and of all such wickedness

74   Is all my preaching, thus to make them free

75   With offered pence, the which pence come to me.

76   For my intent is only pence to win,

77   And not at all for punishment of sin.

78   When they are dead, for all I think thereon

79   Their souls may well black-berrying have gone!

80   For, certainly, there's many a sermon grows

81   Ofttimes from evil purpose, as one knows;

82   Some for folks' pleasure and for flattery,

83   To be advanced by all hypocrisy,

84   And some for vainglory, and some for hate.

85   For, when I dare not otherwise debate,

86   Then do I sharpen well my tongue and sting

87   The man in sermons, and upon him fling

88   My lying **defamations**, if but he

89   Has wronged my brethren or—much worse—wronged me.

90   For though I mention not his proper name,

91   Men know whom I refer to, all the same,

92   By signs I make and other circumstances.

93   Thus I pay those who do us displeasances.

94   Thus spit I out my venom under hue

95   Of holiness, to seem both good and true.

96   "But briefly my intention I'll express;

97   I preach no sermon, save for covetousness.

98   For that my theme is yet, and ever was,

99   *'Radix malorum est cupiditas.'*

100   Thus can I preach against that self-same vice

101   Which I indulge, and that is avarice.

102   But though myself be guilty of that sin,

103   Yet can I cause these other folk to win

104   From avarice and really to repent.

105   But that is not my principal intent.

106   I preach no sermon, save for covetousness;

107   This should suffice of that, though, as I guess.

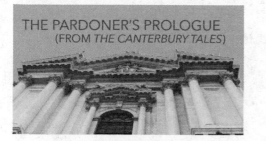

THE PARDONER'S PROLOGUE
(FROM *THE CANTERBURY TALES*)

First Read

Read "The Pardoner's Prologue." After you read, complete the Think Questions below.

☁ THINK QUESTIONS

1. In stanza two, the Pardoner says, "Our liege-lord's seal on my patent perfect, / I show that first, my safety to protect, / And then no man's so old, no priest nor clerk, / As to disturb me in Christ's holy work." What can you infer about the Pardoner's attitude about the bulls, or official public decrees, that he carries? What purpose do they serve for him? Cite evidence from the text to support your explanation.

2. What are the two relics, or religious objects imbued with miraculous powers, that the Pardoner discusses? What are the specific alleged powers of these seemingly banal objects, according to the Pardoner? Cite evidence from the text to support your answer.

3. Citing the Pardoner's own words, what do you think he is most concerned about? How deeply is he invested in the salvation of his congregants?

4. The Latin word *pater* means "father." With this information in mind and using context clues from the text, write your best definition of the word **patriarch** here.

5. What is the meaning of the word **avarice** as it is used in the text? Write your best definition here, along with a brief explanation of how you arrived at its meaning.

Please note that excerpts and passages in the StudySync® library and this workbook are intended as touchstones to generate interest in an author's work. The excerpts and passages do not substitute for the reading of entire texts, and StudySync® strongly recommends that students seek out and purchase the whole literary or informational work in order to experience it as the author intended. Links to online resellers are available in our digital library. In addition, complete works may be ordered through an authorized reseller by filling out and returning to StudySync® the order form enclosed in this workbook.

Reading & Writing
Companion

71

Skill:
Point of View

Use the Checklist to analyze Point of View in "The Pardoner's Prologue." Refer to the sample student annotations about Point of View in the text.

••• CHECKLIST FOR POINT OF VIEW

To grasp a character's point of view in which what is directly stated is different from what is really meant, note the following:

✓ Literary techniques intended to provide humor or criticism. Examples of these include:

- Sarcasm or the use of language that says one thing, but means the opposite.

- Irony or a contrast between what one expects to happen and what happens.

- Understatement or an instance where a character deliberately makes a situation seem less important or serious than it is.

- Satire or the use of humor, irony, exaggeration, or ridicule to expose and criticize people's foolishness or vices.

✓ Possible critiques an author might be making about contemporary society through theme or characters' actions and words.

✓ An unreliable narrator or character whose point of view cannot be trusted.

To analyze a case in which grasping a point of view requires distinguishing what is directly stated in a text from what is really meant, consider the following questions:

✓ When do you notice that the reader's point of view differs from that of the character or speaker in this text?

✓ How does a character's or narrator's point of view contribute to a non-literal understanding of the text?

✓ How does the use of sarcasm, understatement, or satire add meaning to the story?

✓ How does the author use these techniques to expose or criticize some aspect of society?

Skill:
Point of View

Reread lines 14–43 from "The Pardoner's Prologue." Then, using the Checklist on the previous page, answer the multiple-choice questions below.

⟳ YOUR TURN

1. The Pardoner uses figurative language when he states "To spice therewith a bit my sermoning / And stir men to devotion, marvelling. . ." Why does the Pardoner use this metaphor?

   - ○ A. He uses the metaphor to explain how he makes his sermons more appetizing so he can better trick the churchgoers.
   - ○ B. He uses the metaphor to explain the process of using potions and relics in the forgiveness of sin.
   - ○ C. The metaphor serves to educate the churchgoers.
   - ○ D. He uses the metaphor to persuade the churchgoers.

2. Which of the following phrases make it clear that the Pardoner knows he is a liar?

   - ○ A. "And, good sirs, it's a cure for jealousy;"
   - ○ B. "Shall every sheep be healed that of this well / Drinks but one draught"
   - ○ C. "Then show I forth my hollow crystal-stones,"
   - ○ D. "Relics are these, as they think, every one"

3. This question has two parts. First, answer Part A. Then, answer Part B.

   Part A: Which statement best reflects the relationship the Pardoner has with the churchgoers?

   - ○ A. He respects them and seeks their advice on religious matters.
   - ○ B. He tries to manipulate them and hide his true intentions.
   - ○ C. He tries to help them but is concerned they won't accept it.
   - ○ D. He believes they are intelligent but immoral.

Please note that excerpts and passages in the StudySync® library and this workbook are intended as touchstones to generate interest in an author's work. The excerpts and passages do not substitute for the reading of entire texts, and StudySync® strongly recommends that students seek out and purchase the whole literary or informational work in order to experience it as the author intended. Links to online resellers are available in our digital library. In addition, complete works may be ordered through an authorized reseller by filling out and returning to StudySync® the order form enclosed in this workbook.

Reading & Writing Companion 73

Part B: Which of the following quotes from the text BEST supports the answer in Part A?

- ○ A. "Then show I forth my hollow crystal-stones, / Which are crammed full of rags, aye, and of bones; / Relics are these, as they think, every one."

- ○ B. "Then I've in latten box a shoulder bone / Which came out of a holy Hebrew's sheep."

- ○ C. "If this bone shall be washed in any well, / Then if a cow, calf, sheep, or ox should swell That's eaten snake, or been by serpent stung, / Take water of that well and wash its tongue."

- ○ D. "As that Jew taught of yore in his priestcraft, / His beasts and all his store shall multiply."

Skill:
Connotation and Denotation

Use the Checklist to analyze Connotation and Denotation in "The Pardoner's Prologue." Refer to the sample student annotations about Connotation and Denotation in the text.

••• CHECKLIST FOR CONNOTATION AND DENOTATION

In order to identify the denotative meanings of words, use the following steps:

✓ first, note unfamiliar words and phrases, key words used to describe important characters, events, and ideas, or words that inspire an emotional reaction

✓ next, determine and note the denotative meaning of words by consulting a reference material such as a dictionary, glossary, or thesaurus

✓ finally, analyze nuances in the meaning of words with similar denotations

To better understand the meaning of words and phrases as they are used in a text, including connotative meanings, use the following questions as a guide:

✓ What is the genre or subject of the text? Based on context, what do you think the meaning of the word is intended to be?

✓ Is your inference the same or different from the dictionary definition?

✓ Does the word create a positive, negative, or neutral emotion?

✓ What synonyms or alternative phrasing help you describe the connotative meaning of the word?

To determine the meaning of words and phrases as they are used in a text, including connotative meanings, use the following questions as a guide:

✓ What is the denotative meaning of the word? Is that denotative meaning correct in context?

✓ What possible positive, neutral, or negative connotations might the word have, depending on context?

✓ What textual details signal a particular connotation for the word?

Skill:
Connotation and Denotation

Reread lines 68–79 from "The Pardoner's Prologue." Then, using the Checklist on the previous page, answer the multiple-choice questions below.

↻ YOUR TURN

1. In line 70, the metaphor, "As does a dove that's sitting on a barn," connotes:

   ○ A. the churchgoers are naive and easily duped by the pardoner's false sermons,

   ○ B. the churchgoers are commoners who require the guidance of the more-educated pardoner.

   ○ C. the pardoner is a nuisance who annoys churchgoers by continually asking for donations.

   ○ D. the pardoner is a greedy figure who is swindling churchgoers by trying to seem innocent.

2. What does "When they are dead, for all I think thereon," suggest about the Pardoner?

   ○ A. It suggests the Pardoner's job is finished once someone dies.

   ○ B. It suggests the Pardoner is ignorant when it comes to matters related to death and dying.

   ○ C. It suggests the Pardoner does not care about the souls of his followers.

   ○ D. It suggests the Pardoner participates in burial rites.

3. This question has two parts. First, answer Part A. Then, answer Part B.

   Part A: Which sentence best describes the Pardoner's attitude toward the churchgoers?

   ○ A. He is very concerned about helping the churchgoers go to heaven.

   ○ B. He does not really care whether the churchgoers go to heaven.

   ○ C. He is very concerned about helping the churchgoers become good citizens.

   ○ D. He does not really care whether the churchgoers become good citizens.

   Part B: Which of the following quotes from the text best supports the answer in Part A?

   ○ A. "And east and west upon the folk I beck"

   ○ B. "With hands and swift tongue, then, do I so yarn / That it's a joy to see my busyness."

   ○ C. "When they are dead, for all I think thereon / Their souls may well black-berrying have gone!"

   ○ D. "For my intent is only pence to win, / And not at all for punishment of sin."

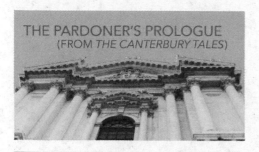

THE PARDONER'S PROLOGUE
(FROM *THE CANTERBURY TALES*)

Close Read

Reread "The Pardoner's Prologue." As you reread, complete the Skills Focus questions below. Then use your answers and annotations from the questions to help you complete the Write activity.

◎ SKILLS FOCUS

1. Sometimes, a character is not completely clear on what they themselves think, and they are wrestling with more than one opinion or point of view. Identify a moment in the text where the Pardoner seems to believe one thing, and then identify a moment in the text where he seems to believe another. Explain why you chose these two passages.

2. Situational irony occurs when the outcome of a situation is the opposite of what was expected. Identify the outcome of the Pardoner's sermons, and explain why it is ironic.

3. The Pardoner makes his living by selling his relics and services to people who believe in him. How does the Pardoner describe his work? What does this reveal about him and what he thinks of his job in the church? Highlight specific words in the text and explain how these words reveal his opinion of the church and his work.

4. The Pardoner tells this story while on a pilgrimage. How does his context — a long journey to a religious destination — cause him to reflect on his true self?

✏ WRITE

MONOLOGUE: In "The Pardoner's Prologue," Chaucer satirizes medieval society by highlighting the greediness of a church official who shamelessly tries to swindle people, convincing them to give him money in exchange for pardons. Think of today's society and imagine a person who represents some sort of corruption or foolishness. Then, write a short satirical monologue to expose that person's true motives.

The English Renaissance

Introduction

This introduction to English Renaissance literature provides readers with the historical and cultural context of the period. The Renaissance movement, inspired by the reign of Queen Elizabeth I and humanist ideals, gave rise to one of the most prolific writers in the English language: William Shakespeare. It was a time in which human experience had more value than ever before. Independent thought, along with scientific and artistic endeavors, were more and more common, contributing to an inspiring culture in which Shakespeare could craft his legendary dramas. Meaning "rebirth" in French, the Renaissance gave birth to some of the most memorable and influential works in the English canon.

"To the humanists, human endeavor had dignity and worth in its own right."

NOTES

1 In May of 2018, Nielsen reported that 29.2 million Americans watched the wedding of Prince Henry and Meghan Markle. Seven years earlier, 22.8 million Americans tuned in to watch Harry's older brother, William, marry Kate Middleton. Why are so many Americans still interested in the royal family nearly 250 years after the United States broke free from British control? The British royals remain international tastemakers. People from all around the world try to emulate their style and preferences. That remains as true today as it was during the seventeenth century, when the tastes of royals like Queen Elizabeth I helped artistic movements gain fans both at home and abroad.

Tudor England

2 The **Tudors** reigned between the fifteenth and seventeenth centuries in England. The first **monarch** of the Tudor dynasty, Henry VII, came into power in 1485. Henry earned the English crown after defeating Richard III, ending the 30-year civil war known as the War of the Roses. His son, Henry VIII, ruled following Henry VII's death in 1509. Three of Henry VIII's children sat on the English throne between 1547 and 1603. Edward VI immediately succeeded his father. After Edward died of tuberculosis, Mary I ruled for a mere five years before her own death. Mary's rule was brief but intense. She received the nickname "Bloody Mary" due to her persecution of Protestants in an attempt to restore Catholicism as the state religion. Elizabeth I reversed this position when she took control of the country in 1558. Despite the religious and political conflicts that divided the Tudors, by the time Elizabeth took the crown a burst of creative energy brought a golden age of culture to England.

Queen Elizabeth

3 Many people celebrated Elizabeth I's ascension to the throne, which restored peace after Mary I's short, turbulent reign. During her reign, Elizabeth was praised for her wit, eloquence, and intellect. Unlike other girls and young women of the time, Elizabeth received a strong formal education. As a result, she was well-versed in many subjects, including mathematics, history, geography, and astronomy, and literate in Greek, Latin, and several other modern languages.

4   Elizabeth's reign was long and eventful. During her 45 years on the throne, she overcame numerous challenges that came from religious conflicts, political intrigue, and threats of war. Many believed that a queen could not rule successfully without a king by her side, but Elizabeth never married. Instead, she proved herself to be more than capable of facing international crises and defending her country. Under Elizabeth's guidance, England became a great sea power capable of defeating its enemies, including the powerful Spanish **Armada** sent by Philip II in an attempt to seize control of England. Additionally, Elizabeth supported a flourishing period of cultural achievement that came to be known as the English **Renaissance**.

Painting of the Spanish Armada in the collection of the National Maritime Museum, Greenwich, England

The Renaissance

5   Spanning the fourteenth and seventeenth centuries, the Renaissance was a vast artistic and cultural movement that started in Italy and spread across Europe. French for "rebirth," the Renaissance marks a period of time between the Middle Ages and the modern world in which there was renewed interest in the sciences and art. During this time, a movement called **humanism** began to take shape. In general, humanists relished new ideas and shared a lively interest in the affairs of the world. This was a shift from medieval art that focused on the afterlife and other religious themes.

6   Humanists also emphasized the ability of the individual to think independently, without guidance from higher authorities. Inspired by political, scientific, and philosophical questions, humanists sought to better understand their own world. During this time period, people painted, sculpted, and composed music as never before as they found their own voices and began to express their own ideas. The value that humanism placed on human experience has permanently altered the way people view and judge the world. For instance,

NOTES

humanism's emphasis on intellectual questioning and direct observation is a forerunner to modern scientific methods.

Shakespeare's Humanism

7   Perhaps no Renaissance writer is more well-known than William Shakespeare. More than 400 years after his death, the poet and playwright is still said to be the world's favorite author. Shakespeare is beloved for both the characters he created and the language he used in his writing. His ability to absorb and transform different kinds of material, ranging from the political issues of his own time to events from Roman and English history, reflects humanist ideals. Shakespeare's tragedies and histories focus on complex individuals who seek to fulfill their full potential while also grappling with painful, difficult dilemmas. At the same time, his comedies are robust with jokes and songs that provide audiences with an escape from their own problems. From Puck to Hamlet and Falstaff to Lady Macbeth, Shakespeare's canon portrays a complete range of human experiences. Young and old, women and men, good and evil, beggars and kings—characters from all walks of life live in Shakespeare's plays.

Ophelia offering fennel and columbines, engraving from
The Illustrated London News, 1892.

Major Concepts

8   • **Humanism**—To the humanists, human endeavor had dignity and worth in its own right. Influenced by this idea, English writers began to shift their focus from religious concerns and concentrate on secular subjects, such as love, politics, science, and philosophy. Later, in the 18th century, a movement called the Enlightenment builds on the ideas of individual dignity, rational thought, and secular law.

   • **A Bard for the Ages**—William Shakespeare was a singular genius who wrote poems and plays that represent the full flowering of the English Renaissance. His characters, seeking to fulfill their potential, are constantly probing and striving, demonstrating their wit at court, displaying their courage on the battlefield, falling in love and writing poetry, or devising plots to bring about their deepest desires, whether loving or vengeful.

Style and Form

Shakespearean Drama

9   • Shakespeare invented little content out of thin air. Instead, he dramatized stories from sources such as Petrarch and Holinshed, often combining elements from multiple accounts of the same story.

• Shakespeare's plays follow a strict format. Each has five acts, and each of those acts contain scenes. Characters express themselves through dialogue as well as soliloquies and monologues. A soliloquy is a speech delivered directly to the audience in which a character reveals his or her innermost thoughts. A monologue is a long speech delivered to another character.

• Subplots, or minor plotlines that support the main plot, are common in Shakespearean drama. Conflicts often arise between characters due to misunderstandings or misinformation that stems from an event that takes place in a subplot.

• Shakespeare's language varies from play to play and sometimes within a play. He is known for writing in iambic pentameter. In this meter, each line has five units, known as feet, and each foot contains an unstressed syllable followed by a stressed syllable. He often uses iambic pentameter to write in blank verse, or writing with a regular meter but without a regular rhyme scheme. He may also include some rhyming couplets for emphasis. However, the language in Shakespeare's plays is not limited to any particular style or meter. He also uses prose, which is ordinary speech without meter or rhyme, when more formal language may seem out of place.

• Sophisticated, intricate language is a trademark of Shakespearean drama. Many plays include elaborate extended metaphors as well as bawdy puns, word play, and double entendres. Humor is always present, even in his tragedies.

10   In addition to featuring characters from all walks of life, Shakespeare's plays drew crowds made up of members from every level of society. Although most of Shakespeare's works were written after her death, there is proof that Queen Elizabeth I watched several of his plays at court. Elizabeth's successor, James I, even became a patron of Shakespeare's theater company, which was renamed The King's Men. With a focus on individual thought and experiences, it is easy to see why Shakespearean drama and other humanist works were so popular during the Renaissance and continue to be valued. How do the ideas introduced and developed through Renaissance literature continue to inspire audiences today?

Literary Focus

Read "Literary Focus: The English Renaissance." After you read, complete the Think Questions below.

☁ THINK QUESTIONS

1. Why was Elizabeth I an important monarch who is still remembered today? Provide two or three reasons, citing evidence from the text to support your response.

2. What were humanists interested in and inspired by? Explain, citing evidence from the text to support your response.

3. Based on the information in the reading, explain what a soliloquy is. Why do you think Shakespeare was able to make this form of dramatic speech so popular during the Renaissance specifically? Use evidence from the text to help support your explanations.

4. Use context clues to determine the meaning of the word **monarch**. Write your definition here, along with the specific words or phrases that helped you come to your conclusion. Then, check a dictionary to confirm your understanding.

5. What is the meaning of the word **armada** as it used in this text? Write your best definition here, in addition to an explanation of how you arrived at the word's meaning.

Shakespeare:
The World as Stage

ARGUMENTATIVE TEXT
Bill Bryson
2007

Introduction

K nown for his distinctly humorous writing style, Bill Bryson (b. 1951) is a highly regarded American author of various nonfiction books on travel, science, language, and other topics. Bryson's biography of William Shakespeare, *Shakespeare: The World as Stage,* focuses on what little is known conclusively about the famous playwright and poet. The excerpt here discusses the Shakespeare authorship debate.

"The presumption is that William Shakespeare of Stratford was, at best, an amiable stooge . . ."

From Chapter 9: Claimants

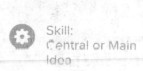

1   There is an extraordinary—seemingly an **insatiable**—urge on the part of quite a number of people to believe that the plays of William Shakespeare were written by someone other than William Shakespeare. The number of published books suggesting—or more often insisting—as much is estimated now to be well over five thousand.

2   Shakespeare's plays, it is held, so brim with expertise—on law, medicine, statesmanship, court life, military affairs, the bounding main, antiquity, life abroad—that they cannot possibly be the work of a single lightly educated **provincial**. The presumption is that William Shakespeare of Stratford was, at best, an amiable **stooge**, an actor who lent his name as cover for someone of greater talent, someone who could not, for one reason or another, be publicly identified as a playwright.

3   The controversy has been given respectful airing in the highest quarters. PBS, the American television network, in 1996 produced an hour-long documentary **unequivocally** suggesting that Shakespeare probably wasn't Shakespeare. *Harper's Magazine* and *The New York Times* have both devoted generous amounts of space to sympathetically considering the anti-Stratford arguments[1]. The Smithsonian Institution in 2002 held a seminar titled "Who Wrote Shakespeare?" The best-read article in the British magazine *History Today* was one examining the authorship question. Even *Scientific American* entered the fray with an article proposing that the person portrayed in the famous Martin Droeshout engraving[2] might actually be—I weep to say it—Elizabeth I. Perhaps the most extraordinary development of all is that Shakespeare's Globe Theater in London—built as a monument for his plays and with aspirations to be a world-class study center—became, under the

Skill:
Central or Main
Idea

Based on the first sentence I know that Bryson's main idea will address the Shakespeare debate. Since he is not referring to himself, I can infer that Bryson does not agree that someone other than Shakespeare created these works.

---

1. **anti-Stratford arguments** referring to the idea that William Shakespeare of Stratford was not the real author of the plays attributed to him
2. **the famous Martin Droeshout engraving** a famous portrait of Shakespeare engraved by Martin Droeshout appearing on the title page of the collection of Shakespeare's plays published in 1623

Copyright © BookheadEd Learning, LLC

NOTES

Skill:
Connotation and Denotation

Bryson calls Wright's description of Shakespeare "wildly imaginative." This is an insult since historians write about facts. In fact, "unimpeachable" means reliable, which tells me he takes issue with Rubinstein's imagination.

Skill:
Informational Text Elements

Bryson uses records from that time period as evidence to support his argument. This record lends credibility and refutes assumptions made by the opposition.

stewardship of the artistic director Mark Rylance, a kind of clearinghouse for anti-Stratford sentiment.

4   So it needs to be said that nearly all of the anti-Shakespeare sentiment—actually all of it, every bit—involves manipulative scholarship or sweeping misstatements of fact. Shakespeare "never owned a book," a writer for *The New York Times* gravely informed readers in one doubting article in 2002. The statement cannot actually be refuted, for we know nothing about his incidental possessions. But the writer might just as well have suggested that Shakespeare never owned a pair of shoes or pants. For all the evidence tells us, he spent his life unclothed as well as bookless, but it is probable that what is lacking is the evidence, not the apparel or the books.

5   Daniel Wright, a professor at Concordia University in Portland, Oregon, and an active anti-Stratfordian, wrote in *Harper's Magazine* that Shakespeare was "a simple, untutored wool and grain merchant" and "a rather ordinary man who had no connection to the literary world." Such statements can only be characterized as wildly imaginative. Similarly, in the normally **unimpeachable** *History Today*, William D. Rubinstein, a professor at the University of Wales at Aberystwyth, stated in the opening paragraph of his anti-Shakespeare survey: "Of the seventy-five known contemporary documents in which Shakespeare is named, not one concerns his career as an author."

6   That is not even close to being so. In the Master of the Revels' accounts for 1604-1605—that is, the record of plays performed before the king, about as official a record as a record can be—Shakespeare is named seven times as the author of plays performed before James I. He is identified on the title pages as the author of the sonnets and in the dedications of two poems. He is named as author on several quarto[3] editions of his plays, by Francis Meres in *Palladis Tamia*, and by Robert Greene in the *Groat's-Worth of Wit*. John Webster identifies him as one of the great playwrights of the age in his preface to *The White Devil.*

7   The only absence among contemporary records is not of documents connecting Shakespeare to his works but of documents connecting any other human being to them. As the Shakespeare scholar Jonathan Bate has pointed out, virtually no one "in Shakespeare's lifetime or for the first two hundred years after his death expressed the slightest doubt about his authorship."

Excerpted from *Shakespeare: The World As Stage* by Bill Bryson, published by HarperCollins Publishers.

---

3. **quarto** a book printed on a full sheet that is folded twice to produce four leaves; Shakespeare's works were published in quarto or folio format (a larger, taller book)

First Read

Read *Shakespeare: The World as Stage*. After you read, complete the Think Questions below.

1. Why does the author list sources of media coverage of the authorship controversy at the beginning of the selection? Cite evidence from the text to support your answer.

2. What is the author's response to the claim that Shakespeare "never owned a book"? What tone does he use in his response? Support your answer with evidence from the text.

3. How does the author conclude this excerpt? What does that tell you about Bryson's view of the authorship debate? Support your inference with evidence from the text.

4. Use context clues to determine the meaning of the word **provincial** as it is used in *Shakespeare: The World as Stage*. Write your definition of *provincial* here and describe how you determined the meaning.

5. Use your knowledge of word parts and the context clues provided in the text to determine the meaning of **unimpeachable**. Write your definition of *unimpeachable* and describe how you determined the meaning.

Please note that excerpts and passages in the StudySync® library and this workbook are intended as touchstones to generate interest in an author's work. The excerpts and passages do not substitute for the reading of entire texts, and StudySync® strongly recommends that students seek out and purchase the whole literary or informational work in order to experience it as the author intended. Links to online resellers are available in our digital library. In addition, complete works may be ordered through an authorized reseller by filling out and returning to StudySync® the order form enclosed in this workbook.

Reading & Writing Companion   87

Skill:
Central or Main Idea

Use the Checklist to analyze Central or Main Idea in *Shakespeare: The World as Stage*. Refer to the sample student annotations about Central or Main Idea in the text.

••• CHECKLIST FOR CENTRAL OR MAIN IDEA

In order to identify two or more central ideas of a text, note the following:

✓ key details in each paragraph or section of text, distinguishing what they have in common

✓ the main idea in each paragraph or group of paragraphs

✓ whether the details contain information that could indicate more than one main idea in a text

- a science text, for example, may provide information about a specific environment and also a message on ecological awareness

- a biography may contain equally important ideas about a person's achievements, influence, and the time period in which the person lives or lived

✓ when each central idea emerges

✓ ways that the central ideas interact and build on one another

To determine two or more central ideas of a text and analyze their development over the course of the text, including how they interact and build on one another to provide a complex analysis, consider the following questions:

✓ What main idea(s) do the details in each paragraphs explain or describe?

✓ What central or main ideas do all the paragraphs support?

✓ How do the central ideas interact and build on one another? How does this affect when they emerge?

✓ How might you provide an objective summary of the text? What details would you include?

Skill:
Central or Main Idea

Reread paragraphs 6 and 7 from *Shakespeare: The World as Stage*. Then, using the Checklist on the previous page, answer the multiple-choice questions below.

♻ YOUR TURN

1. Which of the following sentences best summarizes these two paragraphs?

   ○ A. For two hundred years after Shakespeare's death, no one questioned whether he was the original author of his works.

   ○ B. People who choose to question Shakespeare's authorship are free to do so, but they willfully ignore the facts.

   ○ C. Not only is there historical evidence of Shakespeare's authorship, there also is no historical evidence of anyone else having authored these plays.

   ○ D. Scholars continue to question Shakespeare's authorship, based on growing evidence.

2. Which sentence or phrase from the passage does NOT offer clear evidence supporting Bryson's main idea?

   ○ A. As the Shakespeare scholar Jonathan Bate has pointed out, virtually no one "in Shakespeare's lifetime or for the first two hundred years after his death expressed the slightest doubt about his authorship."

   ○ B. The only absence among contemporary records is not of documents connecting Shakespeare to his works but of documents connecting any other human being to them.

   ○ C. In the Master of the Revels' accounts for 1604–1605 — that is, the record of plays performed before the king, about as official a record as a record can be — Shakespeare is named seven times as the author of plays performed before James I.

   ○ D. He is named as author on several quarto editions of his plays, by Francis Meres in *Palladis Tamia*, and by Robert Greene in the *Groat's-Worth of Wit*.

Reading & Writing Companion

3. In what ways does Bryson mostly develop his main idea?

◯ A. By providing a study of Shakespeare's works and share what he learned with a larger audience.

◯ B. By persuading his audience to become familiar with 17th century literature.

◯ C. By providing evidence of Shakespeare's authorship.

◯ D. By ridiculing those who question Shakespeare's authorship.

Skill:
Connotation and Denotation

Use the Checklist to analyze Connotation and Denotation in *Shakespeare: The World as Stage*. Refer to the sample student annotations about Connotation and Denotation in the text.

••• CHECKLIST FOR CONNOTATION AND DENOTATION

1. In order to identify the denotative meanings of words, use the following steps:

   ✓ first, note unfamiliar words and phrases, key words used to describe important individuals, events, and ideas, or words that inspire an emotional reaction

   ✓ next, determine and note the denotative meaning of words by consulting a reference material such as a dictionary, glossary, or thesaurus

   ✓ finally, analyze nuances in the meaning of words with similar denotations

2. To better understand the meaning of words and phrases as they are used in a text, including connotative meanings, use the following questions as a guide:

   ✓ What is the genre or subject of the text? Based on context, what do you think the meaning of the word is intended to be?

   ✓ Is your inference the same or different from the dictionary definition?

   ✓ Does the word create a positive, negative, or neutral emotion?

   ✓ What synonyms or alternative phrasing help you describe the connotative meaning of the word?

3. To determine the meaning of words and phrases as they are used in a text, including connotative meanings, use the following questions as a guide:

   ✓ What is the denotative meaning of the word? Is that denotative meaning correct in context?

   ✓ What possible positive, neutral, or negative connotations might the word have, depending on context?

   ✓ What textual details signal a particular connotation for the word?

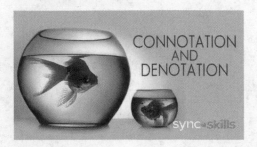

Skill:
Connotation and Denotation

Reread paragraphs 1 and 2 from *Shakespeare: The World as Stage*. Then, using the Checklist on the previous page, answer the multiple-choice questions below.

⟳ YOUR TURN

1. What is the meaning of *insatiable* as it is used in paragraph 1 of the text?

   ○ A. limited
   ○ B. loose
   ○ C. unexplained
   ○ D. relentless

2. Read the following dictionary entry:

   in·sist \In·sist

   verb

   1. demand something forcefully, not accepting refusal.
   2. demand forcefully to have something.
   3. persist in doing something even though it is annoying or odd.

   Decide which definition and explanation best matches *insist* and its connotations in *Shakespeare: A World As Stage*.

   ○ A. As used in paragraph 1, insist means to demand something forcefully.
   ○ B. As used in paragraph 1, insist means to do something even if it is annoying.
   ○ C. As used in paragraph 1, insist means to not accept a refusal.
   ○ D. As used in paragraph 1, insist means to do something odd.

 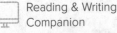

3. Which of the following words used in paragraph 2 most denotes that the author believes anti-Stratfordians are stubborn with their ideas, despite contrary evidence?

○ A. presumption

○ B. greater talent

○ C. publicly

○ D. insisting

Skill:
Informational Text Elements

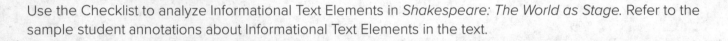

Use the Checklist to analyze Informational Text Elements in *Shakespeare: The World as Stage*. Refer to the sample student annotations about Informational Text Elements in the text.

••• CHECKLIST FOR INFORMATIONAL TEXT ELEMENTS

In order to identify a complex set of ideas or sequence of events, note the following:

✓ key details in the text that provide information about individuals, events, and ideas

✓ interactions between specific individuals, ideas, or events

✓ important developments over the course of the text

✓ transition words and phrases that signal interactions between individuals, events, and ideas, such as *because, as a consequence,* or *as a result.*

✓ similarities and differences between different types of information in the text by comparing and contrasting facts and opinions

To analyze a complex set of ideas or sequence of events and explain how specific individuals, ideas, or events interact and develop over the course of the text, consider the following questions:

✓ How does the order in which ideas or events are presented affect the connections between them?

✓ How do specific individuals, ideas, or events interact and develop over the course of the text?

✓ What other features, if any, help you to analyze the events, ideas, or individuals in the text?

Skill:
Informational Text Elements

Reread paragraphs 4 and 5 from *Shakespeare: The World as Stage*. Then, using the Checklist on the previous page, answer the multiple-choice questions below.

⟳ YOUR TURN

1. When the author states that "The statement cannot actually be refuted," he means—

   ○ A. To acknowledge the lack of information about Shakespeare.

   ○ B. There is no evidence, only assumption and opinion to support the notion that Shakespeare never owned a book.

   ○ C. To persuade the reader to make assumptions about Shakespeare.

   ○ D. To manipulate scholarly opinion on the subject.

2. What is most likely the reason Bryson provides various examples of anti-Shakespearean sentiment?

   ○ A. To evoke emotion.

   ○ B. To create confusion among complex ideas.

   ○ C. To educate the reader on the subject matter.

   ○ D. To explain opposing viewpoints and refute claims.

3. In paragraph 5, the author tells us that Daniel Wright is a "professor at Concordia University in Portland, Oregon and an active anti-Stratfordian." What function does this information play within the text?

   ○ A. To establish Wright as a credible source on Shakespeare.

   ○ B. To include a member of academia in his essay.

   ○ C. To present Wright's professional details in order to later refute his opinion-based claims.

   ○ D. To present a scholarly opinion in support of the author's claim.

Close Read

Reread *Shakespeare: The World as Stage*. As you reread, complete the Skills Focus questions below. Then use your answers and annotations from the questions to help you complete the Write activity.

◎ SKILLS FOCUS

1. What is Bryson's central idea in Paragraph 4? How does Bryson's tone in the paragraph help develop the central idea? Highlight evidence to support your ideas and use the annotation tool to write your response.

2. In the second paragraph, what does Bryson mean when he refers to Shakespeare as a "lightly educated provincial"? What connotation does that phrase have, and what does it tell you about Bryson's viewpoint? Highlight evidence in the text and use the annotation tool to explain the phrase.

3. Why does Bryson list the professions of Daniel Wright and William D. Rubinstein in Paragraph 5? What is his purpose for including the long list of media outlets in Paragraph 3? How do these details support his central idea? Highlight evidence from the text and make annotations to support your ideas.

4. Identify an opposing opinion Bryson considers, and the argument he forges in response. Explain how his rebuttal contributes to the effectiveness of the text. How does it support his main idea? Cite evidence from the text to support your answer.

5. What are the truths about Shakespeare and the scholarship surrounding Shakespeare that the author is defending in this excerpt? Why does this truth matter?

✎ WRITE

ANALYSIS: Bryson takes a strong, transparent view on the subject of Shakespearean authorship from the beginning of the excerpt, and maintains it throughout. What is Bryson's main idea regarding the authorship debate? What are the key pieces of evidence and structures he uses to make his point? Cite specific evidence from the text to support of your claim.

Hamlet and His Problems

ARGUMENTATIVE TEXT
T. S. Eliot
1919

Introduction

Written in 1919, this essay by writer T. S. Eliot (1888–1965) urges critics to analyze *Hamlet* through the lens of New Criticism, which views a text outside its history or performance. Eliot's essay addresses the concept of finding the "objective correlative," a technique used to evoke emotion in an audience.

"The grounds of *Hamlet's* failure are not immediately obvious."

1   Few critics have even admitted that *Hamlet* the play is the primary problem, and Hamlet the character only secondary. And Hamlet the character has had an especial temptation for that most dangerous type of critic: the critic with a mind which is naturally of the creative order, but which through some weakness in creative power exercises itself in criticism instead. These minds often find in Hamlet a **vicarious** existence for their own artistic realization. Such a mind had Goethe, who made of Hamlet a Werther; and such had Coleridge, who made of Hamlet a Coleridge; and probably neither of these men in writing about Hamlet remembered that his first business was to study a work of art. The kind of criticism that Goethe and Coleridge produced, in writing of Hamlet, is the most misleading kind possible. For they both possessed unquestionable critical insight, and both make their critical aberrations the more plausible by the substitution—of their own Hamlet for Shakespeare's—which their creative gift effects. We should be thankful that Walter Pater did not fix his attention on this play.

T. S. Eliot, 1951

2   Two recent writers, Mr. J. M. Robertson and Professor Stoll of the University of Minnesota, have issued small books which can be praised for moving in the other direction. Mr. Stoll performs a service in recalling to our attention the labours of the critics of the seventeenth and eighteenth centuries, observing that they knew less about psychology than more recent Hamlet critics, but they were nearer in spirit to Shakespeare's art; and as they insisted on the importance of the effect of the whole rather than on the importance of the leading character, they were nearer, in their old-fashioned way, to the secret of dramatic art in general.

3   *Qua*[1] work of art, the work of art cannot be interpreted; there is nothing to interpret; we can only criticize it according to standards, in comparison to

---

1. **Qua** (Latin) as being

other works of art; and for "interpretation" the chief task is the presentation of relevant historical facts which the reader is not assumed to know. Mr. Robertson points out, very pertinently, how critics have failed in their "interpretation" of Hamlet by ignoring what ought to be very obvious: that *Hamlet* is a **stratification**, that it represents the efforts of a series of men, each making what he could out of the work of his predecessors. The *Hamlet* of Shakespeare will appear to us very differently if, instead of treating the whole action of the play as due to Shakespeare's design, we perceive his *Hamlet* to be superposed upon much cruder material which persists even in the final form.

4   We know that there was an older play by Thomas Kyd, that extraordinary dramatic (if not poetic) genius who was in all probability the author of two plays so dissimilar as the *Spanish Tragedy* and *Arden of Feversham;* and what this play was like we can guess from three clues: from the *Spanish Tragedy* itself, from the tale of Belleforest upon which Kyd's *Hamlet* must have been based, and from a version acted in Germany in Shakespeare's lifetime which bears strong evidence of having been adapted from the earlier, not from the later, play. From these three sources it is clear that in the earlier play the motive was a revenge-motive simply; that the action or delay is caused, as in the *Spanish Tragedy*, solely by the difficulty of assassinating a monarch surrounded by guards; and that the "madness" of Hamlet was feigned in order to escape suspicion, and successfully. In the final play of Shakespeare, on the other hand, there is a motive which is more important than that of revenge, and which explicitly "blunts" the latter; the delay in revenge is unexplained on grounds of necessity or expediency; and the effect of the "madness" is not to lull but to arouse the king's suspicion. The alteration is not complete enough, however, to be convincing. Furthermore, there are verbal parallels so close to the *Spanish Tragedy* as to leave no doubt that in places Shakespeare was merely *revising* the text of Kyd. And finally there are unexplained scenes—the Polonius-Laertes and the Polonius-Reynaldo scenes—for which there is little excuse; these scenes are not in the verse style of Kyd, and not beyond doubt in the style of Shakespeare. These Mr. Robertson believes to be scenes in the original play of Kyd reworked by a third hand, perhaps Chapman, before Shakespeare touched the play. And he concludes, with very strong show of reason, that the original play of Kyd was, like certain other revenge plays, in two parts of five acts each. The upshot of Mr. Robertson's examination is, we believe, irrefragable: that Shakespeare's *Hamlet,* so far as it is Shakespeare's, is a play dealing with the effect of a mother's guilt upon her son, and that Shakespeare was unable to impose this motive successfully upon the **"intractable"** material of the old play.

5   Of the intractability there can be no doubt. So far from being Shakespeare's masterpiece, the play is most certainly an artistic failure. In several ways the

NOTES

play is puzzling, and disquieting as is none of the others. Of all the plays it is the longest and is possibly the one on which Shakespeare spent most pains; and yet he has left in it **superfluous** and inconsistent scenes which even hasty revision should have noticed. The versification is variable. Lines like:

6   Look, the morn, in russet mantle clad,
Walks o'er the dew of yon high eastern hill,

7   are of the Shakespeare of *Romeo and Juliet*. The lines in Act v. sc. ii.,

8   Sir, in my heart there was a kind of fighting
That would not let me sleep. . .
Up from my cabin,
My sea-gown scarf'd about me, in the dark
Grop'd I to find out them: had my desire;
Finger'd their packet;

9   are of his quite mature. Both workmanship and thought are in an unstable condition. We are surely justified in attributing the play, with that other profoundly interesting play of "intractable" material and astonishing versification, *Measure for Measure,* to a period of crisis, after which follow the tragic successes which culminate in *Coriolanus. Coriolanus* may be not as "interesting" as *Hamlet,* but it is, with *Antony and Cleopatra,* Shakespeare's most assured artistic success. And probably more people have thought *Hamlet* a work of art because they found it interesting, than have found it interesting because it is a work of art. It is the "Mona Lisa" of literature.

10   The grounds of *Hamlet's* failure are not immediately obvious. Mr. Robertson is undoubtedly correct in concluding that the essential emotion of the play is the feeling of a son towards a guilty mother:

11   "[Hamlet's] tone is that of one who has suffered tortures on the score of his mother's degradation. . . . The guilt of a mother is an almost intolerable motive for drama, but it had to be maintained and emphasized to supply a psychological solution, or rather a hint of one."

12   This, however, is by no means the whole story. It is not merely the "guilt of a mother" that cannot be handled as Shakespeare handled the suspicion of Othello, the infatuation of Antony, or the pride of Coriolanus. The subject might conceivably have expanded into a tragedy like these, intelligible, self-complete, in the sunlight. *Hamlet,* like the sonnets, is full of some stuff that the writer could not drag to light, contemplate, or manipulate into art. And when we search for this feeling, we find it, as in the sonnets, very difficult to localize. You cannot point to it in the speeches; indeed, if you examine the two famous soliloquies you see the versification of Shakespeare, but a content which

might be claimed by another, perhaps by the author of the *Revenge of Bussy d'Ambois,* Act v. sc. i. We find Shakespeare's *Hamlet* not in the action, not in any quotations that we might select, so much as in an unmistakable tone which is unmistakably not in the earlier play.

13 The only way of expressing emotion in the form of art is by finding an "objective correlative"; in other words, a set of objects, a situation, a chain of events which shall be the formula of that *particular* emotion; such that when the external facts, which must terminate in sensory experience, are given, the emotion is immediately evoked. If you examine any of Shakespeare's more successful tragedies, you will find this exact equivalence; you will find that the state of mind of Lady Macbeth walking in her sleep has been communicated to you by a skilful accumulation of imagined sensory impressions; the words of Macbeth on hearing of his wife's death strike us as if, given the sequence of events, these words were automatically released by the last event in the series. The artistic "inevitability" lies in this complete adequacy of the external to the emotion; and this is precisely what is deficient in *Hamlet*. Hamlet (the man) is dominated by an emotion which is inexpressible, because it is in excess of the facts as they appear. And the supposed identity of Hamlet with his author is genuine to this point: that Hamlet's bafflement at the absence of objective equivalent to his feelings is a prolongation of the bafflement of his creator in the face of his artistic problem. Hamlet is up against the difficulty that his disgust is occasioned by his mother, but that his mother is not an adequate equivalent for it; his disgust envelops and exceeds her. It is thus a feeling which he cannot understand; he cannot objectify it, and it therefore remains to poison life and obstruct action. None of the possible actions can satisfy it; and nothing that Shakespeare can do with the plot can express Hamlet for him. And it must be noticed that the very nature of the *données*[2] of the problem precludes objective equivalence. To have heightened the criminality of Gertrude would have been to provide the formula for a totally different emotion in Hamlet; it is just *because* her character is so negative and insignificant that she arouses in Hamlet the feeling which she is incapable of representing.

14 The "madness" of Hamlet lay to Shakespeare's hand; in the earlier play a simple **ruse**, and to the end, we may presume, understood as a ruse by the audience. For Shakespeare it is less than madness and more than feigned. The levity of Hamlet, his repetition of phrase, his puns, are not part of a deliberate plan of dissimulation, but a form of emotional relief. In the character Hamlet it is the buffoonery of an emotion which can find no outlet in action; in the dramatist it is the buffoonery of an emotion which he cannot express in art. The intense feeling, ecstatic or terrible, without an object or exceeding its object, is something which every person of sensibility has known; it is

---

2. **données** (French) basic facts

doubtless a study to pathologists. It often occurs in adolescence: the ordinary person puts these feelings to sleep, or trims down his feeling to fit the business world; the artist keeps it alive by his ability to intensify the world to his emotions. The Hamlet of Laforgue is an adolescent; the Hamlet of Shakespeare is not, he has not that explanation and excuse. We must simply admit that here Shakespeare tackled a problem which proved too much for him. Why he attempted it at all is an insoluble puzzle; under compulsion of what experience he attempted to express the inexpressibly horrible, we cannot ever know. We need a great many facts in his biography; and we should like to know whether, and when, and after or at the same time as what personal experience, he read Montaigne, II. xii., *Apologie de Raimond Sebond*. We should have, finally, to know something which is by hypothesis unknowable, for we assume it to be an experience which, in the manner indicated, exceeded the facts. We should have to understand things which Shakespeare did not understand himself.

✏ WRITE

EXPLANATORY ESSAY: In the essay "Hamlet and His Problems," T. S. Eliot makes the claim that Shakespeare's play *Hamlet* is "an artistic failure." Why does he make this claim? What ideas and examples does he use to support this claim? Write a response in which you answer these questions. Remember to use evidence from the text to support your response.

Hamlet
(Scenes from Acts I, II, III)

DRAMA
William Shakespeare
1601

Introduction

*T*he *Tragedy of Hamlet, Prince of Denmark* by William Shakespeare (ca. 1564–1616) is a vivid portrayal of madness, rich with themes of treachery and revenge. His father the King's death, and his mother's immediate remarriage to his uncle throws Hamlet into existential turmoil—a struggle for personal meaning and grueling internal strife that threatens to consume him. A ghost, once played by Shakespeare himself around 1602, visits the Prince. Hamlet's soliloquies, exemplifying the best of Shakespeare's eloquent and clever language, raise unanswerable questions and explore the reality of being human in one of the greatest plays ever written.

"To be, or not to be, that is the question . . ."

1   *Hamlet has returned home from studying in Wittenberg to attend his father's funeral. Still in deep mourning, Hamlet is appalled by his mother's hasty remarriage to the dead King's brother, who has assumed the throne and persists in calling him "son." The circumstances drive Hamlet to voice his first passionate soliloquy.*

From Act I, Scene ii:

Hamlet: son to the late King Hamlet, and nephew to the present King
Claudius: King of Denmark
Gertrude: Queen of Denmark, and mother to Hamlet
Polonius: Lord Chamberlain
Laertes: son to Polonius

Location: Elsinore, the castle

2   KING: Take thy fair hour, Laertes, time be thine,
3   And thy best graces spend it at thy will!
4   But now, my cousin Hamlet, and my son—

5   HAMLET: *[Aside]* A little more than kin, and less than kind.

6   KING: How is it that the clouds still hang on you?

7   HAMLET: Not so, my lord, I am too much in the sun.

8   QUEEN: Good Hamlet, cast thy nighted color off,
9   And let thine eye look like a friend on Denmark.
10 Do not for ever with thy vailed lids
11 Seek for thy noble father in the dust.
12 Thou know'st 'tis common, all that lives must die,
13 Passing through nature to eternity.

14 HAMLET: Ay, madam, it is common.

Skill:
Dramatic Elements and Structure

The aside reveals Hamlet's negative feelings toward his uncle that motivate him to want to avenge his father's death later in the play.

Also, the author's use of an aside creates a relationship between the audience and Hamlet.

NOTES

15   QUEEN: If it be,
16   Why seems it so particular with thee?

17   HAMLET: Seems, madam? Nay, it is, I know not "seems."
18   'Tis not alone my inky cloak, good mother,
19   Nor customary suits of solemn black,
20   Nor windy suspiration of forc'd breath,
21   No, nor the fruitful river in the eye,
22   Nor the dejected havior of the visage,
23   Together with all forms, moods, shapes of grief,
24   That can denote me truly. These indeed seem,
25   For they are actions that a man might play,
26   But I have that within which passes show,
27   These but the **trappings** and the suits of woe.

28   KING: 'Tis sweet and commendable in your nature, Hamlet,
29   To give these mourning duties to your father.
30   But you must know your father lost a father,
31   That father lost, lost his, and the survivor bound
32   In **filial** obligation for some term
33   To do obsequious sorrow. But to persever
34   In obstinate condolement is a course
35   Of impious stubbornness, 'tis unmanly grief,
36   It shows a will most incorrect to heaven,
37   A heart unfortified, or mind impatient,
38   An understanding simple and unschool'd:
39   For what we know must be, and is as common
40   As any the most vulgar thing to sense,
41   Why should we in our peevish opposition
42   Take it to heart? Fie, 'tis a fault to heaven,
43   A fault against the dead, a fault to nature,
44   To reason most absurd, whose common theme
45   Is death of fathers, and who still hath cried,
46   From the first corse till he that died to-day,
47   "This must be so." We pray you, throw to earth
48   This unprevailing woe, and think of us
49   As of a father, for let the world take note
50   You are the most immediate to our throne,
51   And with no less nobility of love
52   Than that which dearest father bears his son
53   Do I impart toward you. For your intent
54   In going back to school in Wittenberg,
55   It is most **retrograde** to our desire,
56   And we beseech you, bend you to remain

Please note that excerpts and passages in the StudySync® library and this workbook are intended as touchstones to generate interest in an author's work. The excerpts and passages do not substitute for the reading of entire texts, and StudySync® strongly recommends that students seek out and purchase the whole literary or informational work in order to experience it as the author intended. Links to online resellers are available in our digital library. In addition, complete works may be ordered through an authorized reseller by filling out and returning to StudySync® the order form enclosed in this workbook.

Reading & Writing
Companion

105

Copyright © Bookheaded Learning, LLC

NOTES

57 Here in the cheer and comfort of our eye,
58 Our chiefest courtier, cousin, and our son.

59 QUEEN: Let not thy mother lose her prayers, Hamlet,
60 I pray thee stay with us, go not to Wittenberg.

61 HAMLET: I shall in all my best obey you, madam.

62 KING: Why, 'tis a loving and a fair reply.
63 Be as ourself in Denmark. Madam, come.
64 This gentle and unforc'd accord of Hamlet
65 Sits smiling to my heart, in grace whereof,
66 No jocund health that Denmark drinks to-day,
67 But the great cannon to the clouds shall tell,
68 And the King's rouse the heaven shall bruit again,
69 Respeaking earthly thunder. Come away.

70 [Flourish. Exeunt all but HAMLET.]

71 HAMLET: O that this too too solid flesh would melt,
72 Thaw and resolve itself into a dew!
73 Or that the Everlasting had not fix'd
74 His canon 'gainst self-slaughter! O God, God,
75 How weary, stale, flat and unprofitable
76 Seem to me all the uses of this world!
77 Fie on't, ah fie! 'tis an unweeded garden
78 That grows to seed, things rank and gross in nature
79 Possess it merely. That it should come to this!
80 But two months dead, nay, not so much, not two.
81 So excellent a king, that was to this
82 Hyperion[1]—to a satyr[2], so loving to my mother
83 That he might not beteem the winds of heaven
84 Visit her face too roughly. Heaven and earth,
85 Must I remember? Why, she would hang on him
86 As if increase of appetite had grown
87 By what it fed on, and yet, within a month—
88 Let me not think on't! Frailty, thy name is woman!—
89 A little month, or ere those shoes were old
90 With which she followed my poor father's body,
91 Like Niobe, all tears—why, she, even she—
92 O, God, a beast that wants discourse of reason

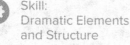

Skill:
Dramatic Elements
and Structure

Alone on stage, Hamlet wishes he were dead because he thinks his life has lost all meaning. His soliloquy and the stage direction work together to reveal how disgusted he is with his mother's marriage to his uncle.

---

1. **Hyperion** the sun-god
2. **satyr** In Greek mythology, a lustful, drunken god of the woods, represented as a half man-half horse or goat.

NOTES

93   Would have mourn'd longer—married with my uncle,
94   My father's brother, but no more like my father
95   Than I to Hercules. Within a month,
96   Ere yet the salt of most unrighteous tears
97   Had left the flushing in her galled eyes,
98   She married—O most wicked speed: to post
99   With such dexterity to incestuous sheets,
100   It is not, nor it cannot come to good,
101   But break my heart, for I must hold my tongue.

From Act II, Scene ii:

102   *Hamlet has been visited by an apparition claiming to be the ghost of his father, who urges Hamlet to avenge his father's murder. Hamlet swears he will obey, but hesitates. Watching a group of traveling players perform the murder of Priam, king of Troy, Hamlet compares one actor's passionate portrayal of Hecuba, Priam's grieving widow, to his own inaction.*

103   HAMLET: O, what a rogue and peasant slave am I!
104   Is it not monstrous that this player here,
105   But in a fiction, in a dream of passion,
106   Could force his soul so to his own conceit
107   That from her working all his visage wann'd,
108   Tears in his eyes, distraction in his aspect,

Hamlet and his father's ghost, by Henry Fuseli.

109   A broken voice, an' his whole function suiting
110   With forms to his conceit? And all for nothing,
111   For Hecuba!
112   What's Hecuba to him, or he to Hecuba,
113   That he should weep for her? What would he do
114   Had he the motive and the cue for passion
115   That I have? He would drown the stage with tears,
116   And cleave the general ear with horrid speech,
117   Make mad the guilty, and appall the free,
118   Confound the ignorant, and amaze indeed
119   The very faculties of eyes and ears. Yet I,
120   A dull and muddy-mettled rascal, peak[3]
121   Like John-a-dreams[4], unpregnant of[5] my cause,

---

3. **peak** to mope
4. **John-a-dreams** a nickname for a daydreamer
5. **unpregnant of** unquickened, or unmoved, by

NOTES

122 And can say nothing; no, not for a king,

123 Upon whose property and most dear life

124 A damn'd defeat was made. Am I a coward?

125 Who calls me villain, breaks my pate across,

126 Plucks off my beard, and blows it in my face,

127 Tweaks me by the nose, gives me the lie i' the throat

128 As deep as to the lungs? Who does me this?

129 Hah, 'swounds, I should take it; for it cannot be

130 But I am pigeon-liver'd, and lack gall

131 To make oppression bitter, or ere this

132 I should 'a' fatted all the region kites

133 With this slave's offal. Bloody, bawdy villain!

134 Remorseless, treacherous, lecherous, kindless villain!

135 Why, what an ass am I! This is most brave,

136 That I, the son of a dear father murthered,

137 Prompted to my revenge by heaven and hell,

138 Must, like a whore unpack my heart with words,

139 And fall a-cursing like a very drab,

140 A stallion. Fie upon't, foh!

141 About, my brains! Hum—I have heard

142 That guilty creatures sitting at a play

143 Have by the very cunning of the scene

144 Been struck so to the soul, that presently

145 They have proclaim'd their malefactions:

146 For murther, though it have no tongue, will speak

147 With most miraculous organ. I'll have these players

148 Play something like the murther of my father

149 Before mine uncle. I'll observe his looks,

150 I'll tent[6] him to the quick. If 'a do blench[7],

151 I know my course. The spirit that I have seen

152 May be the dev'l, and the dev'l hath power

153 T' assume a pleasing shape, yea, and perhaps,

154 Out of my weakness and my melancholy,

155 As he is very potent with such spirits,

156 Abuses me to damn me. I'll have grounds

157 More relative than this—the play's the thing

158 Wherein I'll catch the conscience of the King.

From Act III, Scene i:

159 *Hamlet has been acting mad in front of his family and the court. The King and Polonius hope that Hamlet's strange behavior stems from his love for*

---

6. **tent** probe
7. **blench** flinch

Polonius's daughter, Ophelia, and they spy on the young couple in order to confirm their suspicions. While hidden, they catch Hamlet in a private moment of anguished contemplation.

160 HAMLET: To be, or not to be, that is the question:
161 Whether 'tis nobler in the mind to suffer
162 The slings and arrows of outrageous fortune,
163 Or to take arms against a sea of troubles,
164 And by opposing, end them. To die, to sleep—
165 No more, and by a sleep to say we end
166 The heart-ache and the thousand natural shocks
167 That flesh is heir to; 'tis a consummation
168 Devoutly to be wish'd. To die, to sleep—
169 To sleep, perchance to dream—ay, there's the rub,
170 For in that sleep of death what dreams may come,
171 When we have shuffled off this mortal coil,
172 Must give us pause; there's the respect
173 That makes calamity of so long life:
174 For who would bear the whips and scorns of time,
175 Th' oppressor's wrong, the proud man's contumely,
176 The pangs of despis'd love, the law's delay,
177 The **insolence** of office, and the spurns
178 That patient merit of th' unworthy takes,
179 When he himself might his quietus make
180 With a bare bodkin[8]; who would fardels[9] bear,
181 To grunt and sweat under a weary life,
182 But that the dread of something after death,
183 The undiscover'd country, from whose bourn
184 No traveller returns, puzzles the will,
185 And makes us rather bear those ills we have,
186 Than fly to others that we know not of?
187 Thus conscience does make cowards of us all,
188 And thus the native hue of resolution
189 Is sicklied o'er with the pale cast of thought,
190 And enterprises of great pith and moment
191 With this regard their currents turn awry,
192 And lose the name of action.—Soft you now,
193 The fair Ophelia!—Nymph, in thy orisons[10]
194 Be all my sins remembered.

195 OPHELIA: Good my lord,

---

8. **bare bodkin** mere dagger
9. **fardels** a burden in the form of a bundle
10. **orisons** prayers

Skill: Media

The film shows Hamlet looking at the ocean. His words are heard before he is on screen. He holds a dagger when he says "end them." The film makes Hamlet's suicidal thoughts clearer than I originally read in Shakespeare's words.

NOTES

196   How does your honor for this many a day?

197   HAMLET: I humbly thank you. Well, well, well.

198   OPHELIA: My lord, I have remembrances of yours
199   That I have longèd long to redeliver.
200   I pray you now receive them.

201   HAMLET: No, not I. I never gave you aught.

202   OPHELIA: My honored lord, you know right well you did,
203   And with them, words of so sweet breath composed
204   As made the things more rich. Their perfume lost,
205   Take these again, for to the noble mind
206   Rich gifts wax poor when givers prove unkind.
207   There, my lord.

208   HAMLET: Ha, ha, are you honest?

209   OPHELIA: My lord?

210   HAMLET: Are you fair?

211   OPHELIA: What means your lordship?

212   HAMLET: That if you be honest and fair, your honesty should admit no discourse to your beauty.

213   OPHELIA: Could beauty, my lord, have better commerce than with honesty?

214   HAMLET: Ay, truly, for the power of beauty will sooner transform honesty from what it is to a bawd than the force of honesty can translate beauty into his likeness. This was sometime a paradox, but now the time gives it proof. I did love you once.

215   OPHELIA: Indeed, my lord, you made me believe so.

216   HAMLET: You should not have believed me, for virtue cannot so inoculate our old stock but we shall relish of it. I loved you not.

217   OPHELIA: I was the more deceived.

218   HAMLET: Get thee to a nunnery. Why wouldst thou be a breeder of sinners? I am myself indifferent honest, but yet I could accuse me of such things that it were better my mother had not borne me.

219   I am very proud, revengeful, ambitious, with more offences at my beck than I have thoughts to put them in, imagination to give them shape, or time to act them in. What should such fellows as I do crawling between earth and heaven? We are arrant knaves, all. Believe none of us. Go thy ways to a nunnery. Where's your father?

220   OPHELIA: At home, my lord.

221   HAMLET: Let the doors be shut upon him, that he may play the fool no where but in 's own house. Farewell.

222   OPHELIA: O, help him, you sweet heavens!

223   HAMLET: If thou dost marry, I'll give thee this plague for thy dowry. Be thou as chaste as ice, as pure as snow, thou shalt not escape calumny. Get thee to a nunnery, go. Farewell. Or, if thou wilt needs marry, marry a fool, for wise men know well enough what monsters you make of them. To a nunnery, go, and quickly too. Farewell.

224   OPHELIA: Heavenly powers, restore him!

225   HAMLET: I have heard of your paintings too, well enough. God has given you one face and you make yourselves another. You jig and amble, and you lisp, you nickname God's creatures and make your wantonness your ignorance. Go to, I'll no more on 't. It hath made me mad. I say, we will have no more marriages. Those that are married already, all but one, shall live. The rest shall keep as they are. To a nunnery, go.

226   [Exit HAMLET.]

227   OPHELIA: Oh, what a noble mind is here o'erthrown!—
228   The courtier's, soldier's, scholar's, eye, tongue, sword,
229   Th' expectancy and rose of the fair state,
230   The glass of fashion and the mould of form,
231   Th' observed of all observers, quite, quite down!
232   And I, of ladies most deject and wretched,
233   That sucked the honey of his music vows,
234   Now see that noble and most sovereign reason
235   Like sweet bells jangled, out of tune and harsh;
236   That unmatched form and feature of blown youth
237   Blasted with ecstasy. Oh, woe is me,
238   T' have seen what I have seen, see what I see!

From Act III, Scene iii:

A room in the Castle.

NOTES

239 *[Enter KING, ROSENCRANTZ, and GUILDENSTERN.]*

240 KING: I like him not; nor stands it safe with us
241 To let his madness range. Therefore prepare you;
242 I your commission will forthwith dispatch,
243 And he to England shall along with you:
244 The terms of our estate may not endure
245 Hazard so near us as doth hourly grow
246 Out of his lunacies.

247 GUILDENSTERN: We will ourselves provide:
248 Most holy and religious fear it is
249 To keep those many many bodies safe
250 That live and feed upon your majesty.

251 ROSENCRANTZ: The single and peculiar life is bound,
252 With all the strength and armour of the mind,
253 To keep itself from 'noyance; but much more
254 That spirit upon whose weal depend and rest
255 The lives of many. The cease of majesty
256 Dies not alone; but like a gulf doth draw
257 What's near it with it: it is a massy wheel,
258 Fix'd on the summit of the highest mount,
259 To whose huge spokes ten thousand lesser things
260 Are mortis'd and adjoin'd; which, when it falls,
261 Each small annexment, petty consequence,
262 Attends the **boisterous** ruin. Never alone
263 Did the king sigh, but with a general groan.

264 KING: Arm you, I pray you, to this speedy voyage;
265 For we will fetters put upon this fear,
266 Which now goes too free-footed.

267 ROSENCRANTZ and GUILDENSTERN: We will haste us.

268 *[Exeunt ROSENCRANTZ and GUILDENSTERN.]*

269 *[Enter POLONIUS.]*

270 POLONIUS: My lord, he's going to his mother's closet:
271 Behind the arras I'll convey myself
272 To hear the process; I'll warrant she'll tax him home:
273 And, as you said, and wisely was it said,
274 'Tis meet that some more audience than a mother,
275 Since nature makes them partial, should o'erhear

276 The speech, of vantage. Fare you well, my liege:
277 I'll call upon you ere you go to bed,
278 And tell you what I know.

279 KING: Thanks, dear my lord.

280 *[Exit POLONIUS.]*

281 O, my offence is rank, it smells to heaven;
282 It hath the primal eldest curse upon't,—
283 A brother's murder!—Pray can I not,
284 Though inclination be as sharp as will:
285 My stronger guilt defeats my strong intent;
286 And, like a man to double business bound,
287 I stand In pause where I shall first begin,
288 And both neglect. What if this cursed hand
289 Were thicker than itself with brother's blood,—
290 Is there not rain enough in the sweet heavens
291 To wash it white as snow? Whereto serves mercy
292 But to confront the visage of offence?
293 And what's in prayer but this twofold force,—
294 To be forestalled ere we come to fall,
295 Or pardon'd being down? Then I'll look up;
296 My fault is past. But, O, what form of prayer
297 Can serve my turn? Forgive me my foul murder!—
298 That cannot be; since I am still possess'd
299 Of those effects for which I did the murder,—
300 My crown, mine own ambition, and my queen.
301 May one be pardon'd and retain the offence?
302 In the corrupted currents of this world
303 Offence's gilded hand may shove by justice;
304 And oft 'tis seen the wicked prize itself
305 Buys out the law; but 'tis not so above;
306 There is no shuffling;—there the action lies
307 In his true nature; and we ourselves compell'd,
308 Even to the teeth and forehead of our faults,
309 To give in evidence. What then? what rests?
310 Try what repentance can: what can it not?
311 Yet what can it when one cannot repent?
312 O wretched state! O bosom black as death!
313 O limed soul, that, struggling to be free,
314 Art more engag'd! Help, angels! Make assay:
315 Bow, stubborn knees; and, heart, with strings of steel,

NOTES

⚙ Skill:
Language, Style,
and Audience

The King describes the murder of his brother as so "rank" that the smell rises to heaven. But "my offence is rank" can also mean that the King's "offence," or crime, is to achieve rank.

Reading & Writing
Companion

316 Be soft as sinews of the new-born babe!

317 All may be well.

318 *[Retires and kneels.]*

319 *[Enter Hamlet.]*

320 HAMLET: Now might I do it pat, now he is praying;

321 And now I'll do't;—and so he goes to heaven;

322 And so am I reveng'd.—that would be scann'd:

323 A villain kills my father; and for that,

324 I, his sole son, do this same villain send

325 To heaven.

326 O, this is hire and salary, not revenge.

327 He took my father grossly, full of bread;

328 With all his crimes broad blown, as flush as May;

329 And how his audit stands, who knows save heaven?

330 But in our circumstance and course of thought,

331 'Tis heavy with him: and am I, then, reveng'd,

332 To take him in the purging of his soul,

333 When he is fit and season'd for his passage?

334 No.

335 Up, sword, and know thou a more horrid hent:

336 When he is drunk asleep; or in his rage;

337 Or in the incestuous pleasure of his bed;

338 At gaming, swearing; or about some act

339 That has no relish of salvation in't;—

340 Then trip him, that his heels may kick at heaven;

341 And that his soul may be as damn'd and black

342 As hell, whereto it goes. My mother stays:

343 This physic but prolongs thy sickly days.

344 *[Exit.]*

345 *[The King rises and advances.]*

346 KING: My words fly up, my thoughts remain below:

347 Words without thoughts never to heaven go.

348 *[Exit.]*

First Read

Read *Hamlet*. After you read, complete the Think Questions below.

☁ THINK QUESTIONS

1. In Act I, how do King Claudius and Queen Gertrude try to reason with Hamlet? What does Hamlet's soliloquy suggest about his response to their reasoning? Cite evidence from the text to support your response.

2. In Act II, what key comparison does Hamlet draw between himself and the players, confirming that he is a coward? Cite evidence from the text to support your answer.

3. In Act III, Scene i, what does Hamlet mean when he says, "To be, or not to be, that is the question"? Cite evidence from the text to support your answer.

4. Review the King's lines in Act I, Scene ii, that begin, "Tis sweet and commendable . . ." Use context to determine the meaning of the word **filial** as it is used in the fifth line. Explain how context helped you determine the meaning of the word.

5. Use context clues to determine a preliminary definition of **retrograde**. Write your definition here, and then verify your preliminary definition by checking a dictionary.

Please note that excerpts and passages in the StudySync® library and this workbook are intended as touchstones to generate interest in an author's work. The excerpts and passages do not substitute for the reading of entire texts, and StudySync® strongly recommends that students seek out and purchase the whole literary or informational work in order to experience it as the author intended. Links to online resellers are available in our digital library. In addition, complete works may be ordered through an authorized reseller by filling out and returning to StudySync® the order form enclosed in this workbook.

Reading & Writing Companion

115

Skill:
Dramatic Elements and Structure

Use the Checklist to analyze Dramatic Elements and Structure in *Hamlet*. Refer to the sample student annotations about Dramatic Elements and Structure in the text.

••• CHECKLIST FOR DRAMATIC ELEMENTS AND STRUCTURE

In order to determine the author's choices regarding the development of a drama, note the following:

✓ the names of all the characters, how they are introduced, and their relationships with one another

✓ character development, including personality traits, motivations, decisions each character makes, and the actions they take

✓ the setting(s) of the story and how it influences the characters and the events of the plot

✓ how character choices and dialogue affect the plot

✓ the stage directions and how they are used to reveal character and plot development

To analyze the impact of the author's choices regarding how to develop and relate elements of a story or drama, consider the following questions:

✓ How does the order of events in the play affect the development of the drama?

✓ How are characters introduced, and what does it reveal about them?

✓ In what ways do the characters change over the course of the drama?

✓ How do the choices the characters make help advance the plot?

✓ How does the setting affect the characters and plot?

✓ How do the characters' actions help develop the theme or message of the play?

Skill:
Dramatic Elements and Structure

Reread lines 102–126 from *Hamlet*. Then, using the Checklist on the previous page, answer the multiple-choice questions below.

↻ YOUR TURN

1. This scene is from the second act of Hamlet. The author's choice to use a soliloquy at this point in the play helps advance the plot by —

   ○ A. making the audience approve of Hamlet's plan to get revenge on his family later In the play.

   ○ B. allowing Hamlet's family to find out what he is plotting, which enables them to foil his plan.

   ○ C. creating a mood of forgiveness that will affect Hamlet's actions toward his uncle and mother.

   ○ D. creating tension in the rising action of the play as the audience learns of Hamlet's plan for revenge.

2. The author's choice to use a soliloquy in this part of the play is effective because it —

   ○ A. leaves no question in the audience's mind that Hamlet, alone on stage, is revealing his own inner thoughts and feelings.

   ○ B. allows Hamlet to be alone on stage so that he can tell the audience directly that he enjoys putting on plays.

   ○ C. gives Hamlet a chance to get the audience to react to the claim that he is a rogue and a villain.

   ○ D. gives other actors a chance to be off stage so they can prepare for future scenes.

Please note that excerpts and passages in the StudySync® library and this workbook are intended as touchstones to generate interest in an author's work. The excerpts and passages do not substitute for the reading of entire texts, and StudySync® strongly recommends that students seek out and purchase the whole literary or informational work in order to experience it as the author intended. Links to online resellers are available in our digital library. In addition, complete works may be ordered through an authorized reseller by filling out and returning to StudySync® the order form enclosed in this workbook.

Reading & Writing Companion   117

Skill:
Language, Style, and Audience

Use the Checklist to analyze Language, Style, and Audience in *Hamlet*. Refer to the sample student annotations about Language, Style, and Audience in the text.

••• CHECKLIST FOR LANGUAGE, STYLE, AND AUDIENCE

In order to determine an author's style and possible intended audience, do the following:

✓ identify and define any unfamiliar words or phrases that have multiple meanings

✓ identify language that is particularly fresh, engaging, or beautiful

✓ analyze the surrounding words and phrases as well as the context in which the specific words are being used

✓ note the audience—both intended and unintended—and possible reactions to the author's word choice and style

✓ examine your reaction to the author's word choice and how the author's choice affected your reaction

To analyze the impact of a specific word choice on meaning, including words with multiple meanings or language that is particularly fresh, engaging, or beautiful, consider the following questions:

✓ How does the author's use of fresh, engaging, or beautiful language enhance or change what is being described? How would a specific phrase or sentence sound different or shift in meaning if a synonym were used?

✓ How do the rhyme scheme, meter, and other poetic language affect the meaning?

✓ How does word choice, including different possible meanings from other countries, help determine meaning?

✓ How does Shakespeare use poetic techniques, multiple-meaning words, and language that appeals to emotions to craft a message or idea?

✓ How would the text be different if another type of technique or other words were used?

Reading & Writing Companion

Skill:
Language, Style, and Audience

Reread lines 195–225 from *Hamlet*. Then, using the Checklist on the previous page, answer the multiple-choice questions below.

⟳ YOUR TURN

1. What impact does Hamlet's repeated command of Ophelia to go "to a nunnery" have on the meaning of this scene?

   ○ A. The repetition shows how much Hamlet now regrets having never given anything to Ophelia.
   ○ B. The repetition highlights the tense relationship that Hamlet and Ophelia have always had.
   ○ C. The repetition explains that Hamlet no longer finds Ophelia beautiful.
   ○ D. The repetition reinforces how much Hamlet now distrusts Ophelia.

2. Which statement best explains how the word "fair" is used in this scene?

   ○ A. The word "fair" refers to Ophelia's lack of beauty and judgement.
   ○ B. Hamlet uses the word "fair" to link Ophelia's beauty with what he sees as her lack of honesty.
   ○ C. Hamlet introduces the idea of being "fair" because Ophelia calls his gifts unkind.
   ○ D. The word "fair" refers to the open and honest relationship that Ophelia and Hamlet used to have.

Skill:
Media

Use the Checklist to analyze Media in *Hamlet*. Refer to the sample student annotations about Media in the text.

••• CHECKLIST FOR MEDIA

Before analyzing multiple interpretations of a story, drama, or poem, note the following:

✓ similarities and differences in different media, such as the live production of a play or a recorded novel or poetry

✓ the different time periods and cultures in which the source material and interpretations were produced

To analyze multiple interpretations of a story, drama, or poem, evaluating how each version interprets the source text, consider the following questions:

✓ How does each version interpret the source text? What are the main similarities and differences between the two (or more) versions?

✓ In what ways does the medium affect the interpretations of the source text?

✓ If each version is from a different time period and/or culture, what does each version reveal about the time period and culture in which it was written?

✓ Does information about the time period and culture allow you to make any inferences about the authors' objectives or intentions?

Skill:
Media

Reread lines 169–186 from *Hamlet*. Then, using the Checklist on the previous page, answer the multiple-choice questions below.

↻ YOUR TURN

1. How does Sonnet Man explain the idea of having "To grunt and sweat under a weary life" (line 181)?

   ○ A. Sonnet Man says the line out loud, which helps the listener and viewer know what he means by "a weary life."

   ○ B. Sonnet Man's version shows people fighting to help the listener and viewer see the experiences of someone with "a weary life."

   ○ C. Sonnet Man's version uses voice-over with photographs on the screen to help the listener and viewer understand the line.

   ○ D. Sonnet Man translates the line into his own words to help the listener and viewer understand what he means.

2. Which statement best explains how Sonnet Man interprets Shakespeare's text?

   ○ A. Sonnet Man breaks down the idea of Hamlet having an internal discussion by including the presence of others on the screen.

   ○ B. Sonnet Man's version translates the original words into words more commonly used and understood today.

   ○ C. Sonnet Man's version removes the explicit reference to suicide that was in the original.

   ○ D. Sonnet Man focuses less on Hamlet and more on the other characters in the play.

Please note that excerpts and passages in the StudySync® library and this workbook are intended as touchstones to generate interest in an author's work. The excerpts and passages do not substitute for the reading of entire texts, and StudySync® strongly recommends that students seek out and purchase the whole literary or informational work in order to experience it as the author intended. Links to online resellers are available in our digital library. In addition, complete works may be ordered through an authorized reseller by filling out and returning to StudySync® the order form enclosed in this workbook.

Reading & Writing
Companion

121

Close Read

Reread *Hamlet*. As you reread, complete the Skills Focus questions below. Then use your answers and annotations from the questions to help you complete the Write activity.

1. Identify an important stage direction in Act III, Scene iii, of the play. Explain how this stage direction works together with the dialogue to develop the character of Hamlet.

2. Read lines 312 through 316 in Act III, Scene iii. Knowing that "limed" refers to a bird trapped with a lime-based paste, what do you think Shakespeare suggests, denotatively and connotatively, by using the phrase "limed soul" in line 313?

3. Read lines 75 through 79 of Act I, Scene ii, and explain how the overall meaning of Hamlet's soliloquy is affected by the word choice and tone of these lines.

4. Rewatch the "To be or not to be" speech as interpreted by Laurence Olivier and the Sonnet Man. Explain how Olivier's version is similar to and different from Sonnet Man's version. How do both versions relate back to Shakespeare's version? What does each version of the speech reveal about the time period and culture from which it came?

5. Throughout the play, Hamlet is deeply upset by his challenging situation: his father is dead, and he cannot trust anyone around him. Highlight two moments in which you believe Hamlet reveals his true self amidst these challenges. Explain why you chose these moments, and support your answer with textual evidence from other parts of the excerpt.

✏ WRITE

LITERARY ANALYSIS: A soliloquy is a speech in which a character thinks out loud while alone onstage. Hamlet's three soliloquies in the excerpt offer the reader a window into Hamlet's feelings concerning his father, mother, uncle, and especially himself. How does each soliloquy express Hamlet's conflicted feelings in a unique way? Be sure to use textual evidence to support your analysis.

The Postmaster

FICTION
Rabindranath Tagore
1918

Introduction

A cclaimed Bengali poet, novelist, playwright, and composer, Rabindranath Tagore (1861–1941) was the first non-European Nobel Prize laureate. Today, the Indian, Bangladeshi, and Sri Lankan national anthems are all based on his writings. In "The Postmaster," one of Tagore's most memorable short stories, a postmaster moves from the city of Calcutta to the village of Ulapur and befriends a young orphan. What follows is a moving meditation on the nature of loneliness and love.

"At any rate, the postmaster had but little company; nor had he much to do."

1 The postmaster first took up his duties in the village of Ulapur. Though the village was a small one, there was an indigo factory near by, and the proprietor, an Englishman, had managed to get a post office established.

2 Our postmaster belonged to Calcutta. He felt like a fish out of water in this remote village. His office and living-room were in a dark thatched shed, not far from a green, slimy pond, surrounded on all sides by a dense growth.

Drawing of 19th century Calcutta, India, from a 19th century print, from *The Age We Live In: A History of the Nineteenth Century*

3 The men employed in the indigo factory had no leisure; moreover, they were hardly desirable companions for decent folk. Nor is a Calcutta boy an adept in the art of associating with others. Among strangers he appears either proud or ill at ease. At any rate, the postmaster had but little company; nor had he much to do.

4 At times he tried his hand at writing a verse or two. That the movement of the leaves and the clouds of the sky were enough to fill life with joy—such were the sentiments to which he sought to give expression. But God knows that the poor fellow would have felt it as the gift of a new life, if some genie of the Arabian Nights had in one night swept away the trees, leaves and all, and replaced them with a macadamised road, hiding the clouds from view with rows of tall houses.

5 The postmaster's salary was small. He had to cook his own meals, which he used to share with Ratan, an orphan girl of the village, who did odd jobs for him.

6 When in the evening the smoke began to curl up from the village cowsheds, and the cicalas chirped in every bush; when the mendicants[1] of the Baül sect sang their shrill songs in their daily meeting-place, when any poet, who had attempted to watch the movement of the leaves in the dense bamboo

---

1. **mendicants** members of a religious order who have taken a vow of poverty

Skill: Theme

The postmaster does not enjoy his new setting. He can't appreciate life in the village. It seems he feels isolated and that life here is something to be endured. This suggests isolation is a theme.

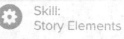

NOTES

thickets, would have felt a ghostly shiver run down his back, the postmaster would light his little lamp, and call out "Ratan."

7   Ratan would sit outside waiting for this call, and, instead of coming in at once, would reply, "Did you call me, sir?"

8   "What are you doing?" the postmaster would ask.

9   "I must be going to light the kitchen fire," would be the answer.

10 And the postmaster would say: "Oh, let the kitchen fire be for awhile; light me my pipe first."

11 At last Ratan would enter, with puffed-out cheeks, vigorously blowing into a flame a live coal to light the tobacco. This would give the postmaster an opportunity of conversing. "Well, Ratan," perhaps he would begin, "do you remember anything of your mother?" That was a fertile subject. Ratan partly remembered, and partly didn't. Her father had been fonder of her than her mother; him she recollected more vividly. He used to come home in the evening after his work, and one or two evenings stood out more clearly than others, like pictures in her memory. Ratan would sit on the floor near the postmaster's feet, as memories crowded in upon her. She called to mind a little brother that she had—and how on some bygone cloudy day she had played at fishing with him on the edge of the pond, with a twig for a make-believe fishing-rod. Such little incidents would drive out greater events from her mind. Thus, as they talked, it would often get very late, and the postmaster would feel too lazy to do any cooking at all. Ratan would then hastily light the fire, and toast some unleavened bread, which, with the cold remnants of the morning meal, was enough for their supper.

12 On some evenings, seated at his desk in the corner of the big empty shed, the postmaster too would call up memories of his own home, of his mother and his sister, of those for whom in his **exile** his heart was sad,—memories which were always haunting him, but which he could not talk about with the men of the factory, though he found himself naturally recalling them aloud in the presence of the simple little girl. And so it came about that the girl would allude to his people as mother, brother, and sister, as if she had known them all her life. In fact, she had a complete picture of each one of them painted in her little heart.

13 One noon, during a break in the rains, there was a cool soft breeze blowing; the smell of the damp grass and leaves in the hot sun felt like the warm breathing of the tired earth on one's body. A persistent bird went on all the afternoon repeating the burden of its one complaint in Nature's audience chamber.

14 The postmaster had nothing to do. The shimmer of the freshly washed leaves, and the banked-up remnants of the retreating rain-clouds were sights to see;

Skill:
Story Elements

Ratan, an orphan, somewhat recalls her parents. She sits on the floor like a favorite pet. This shows how economic setting influences themes of love, loss, and family.

Skill:
Theme

The postmaster is homesick and overwhelmed by memories of his family. This deep connection to his past and his inability to share his feelings with the men in his village show that he is isolated from them but not from the little girl.

and the postmaster was watching them and thinking to himself: "Oh, if only some kindred soul were near—just one loving human being whom I could hold near my heart!" This was exactly, he went on to think, what that bird was trying to say, and it was the same feeling which the murmuring leaves were striving to express. But no one knows, or would believe, that such an idea might also take possession of an ill-paid village postmaster in the deep, silent mid-day interval of his work.

15　The postmaster sighed, and called out "Ratan." Ratan was then sprawling beneath the guava-tree, busily engaged in eating unripe guavas. At the voice of her master, she ran up breathlessly, saying: "Were you calling me, Dada?" "I was thinking," said the postmaster, "of teaching you to read." And then for the rest of the afternoon he taught her the alphabet.

16　Thus, in a very short time, Ratan had got as far as the double consonants.

17　It seemed as though the showers of the season would never end. Canals, ditches, and hollows were all overflowing with water. Day and night the patter of rain was heard, and the croaking of frogs. The village roads became impassable, and marketing had to be done in punts.

18　One heavily clouded morning, the postmaster's little pupil had been long waiting outside the door for her call, but, not hearing it as usual, she took up her dog-eared book, and slowly entered the room. She found her master stretched out on his bed, and, thinking that he was resting, she was about to retire on tip-toe, when she suddenly heard her name—"Ratan!" She turned at once and asked: "Were you sleeping, Dada?" The postmaster in a plaintive voice said: "I am not well. Feel my head; is it very hot?"

19　In the loneliness of his exile, and in the gloom of the rains, his ailing body needed a little tender nursing. He longed to remember the touch on the forehead of soft hands with tinkling bracelets, to imagine the presence of loving womanhood, the nearness of mother and sister. And the exile was not disappointed. Ratan ceased to be a little girl. She at once stepped into the post of mother, called in the village doctor, gave the patient his pills at the proper intervals, sat up all night by his pillow, cooked his gruel for him, and every now and then asked: "Are you feeling a little better, Dada?"

20　It was some time before the postmaster, with weakened body, was able to leave his sick-bed. "No more of this," said he with decision. "I must get a transfer." He at once wrote off to Calcutta an application for a transfer, on the ground of the unhealthiness of the place.

21　Relieved from her duties as nurse, Ratan again took up her old place outside the door. But she no longer heard the same old call. She would sometimes peep inside furtively to find the postmaster sitting on his chair, or stretched on his bed, and staring absent-mindedly into the air. While Ratan was awaiting her call, the postmaster was awaiting a reply to his application. The girl read

her old lessons over and over again,—her great fear was lest, when the call came, she might be found wanting in the double consonants. At last, after a week, the call did come one evening. With an overflowing heart Ratan rushed into the room with her—"Were you calling me, Dada?"

22 The postmaster said: "I am going away to-morrow, Ratan."

23 "Where are you going, Dada?"

24 "I am going home."

25 "When will you come back?"

26 "I am not coming back."

27 Ratan asked no other question. The postmaster, of his own accord, went on to tell her that his application for a transfer had been rejected, so he had **resigned** his post and was going home. For a long time neither of them spoke another word. The lamp went on dimly burning, and from a leak in one corner of the thatch water dripped steadily into an earthen vessel on the floor beneath it.

28 After a while Ratan rose, and went off to the kitchen to prepare the meal; but she was not so quick about it as on other days. Many new things to think of had entered her little brain. When the postmaster had finished his supper, the girl suddenly asked him. "Dada, will you take me to your home?"

29 The postmaster laughed. "What an idea!" said he; but he did not think it necessary to explain to the girl wherein lay the absurdity.

30 That whole night, in her waking and in her dreams, the postmaster's laughing reply haunted her—"What an idea!"

31 On getting up in the morning, the postmaster found his bath ready. He had stuck to his Calcutta habit of bathing in water drawn and kept in pitchers, instead of taking a plunge in the river as was the custom of the village. For some reason or other, the girl could not ask him about the time of his departure, so she had fetched the water from the river long before sunrise, that it should be ready as early as he might want it. After the bath came a call for Ratan. She entered noiselessly, and looked silently into her master's face for orders. The master said: "You need not be anxious about my going away, Ratan; I shall tell my successor to look after you." These words were kindly meant, no doubt: but **inscrutable** are the ways of a woman's heart!

32 Ratan had borne many a scolding from her master without complaint, but these kind words she could not bear. She burst out weeping, and said: "No, no, you need not tell anybody anything at all about me; I don't want to stay on here."

Skill:
Summarizing

Ratan is shocked. Her relationship to him is not valuable enough for him to stay.

This section reminds me of earlier events in the story. The postmaster was never happy in Ulapur.

33   The postmaster was **dumbfounded**. He had never seen Ratan like this before.

34   The new incumbent duly arrived, and the postmaster, having given over charge, prepared to depart. Just before starting he called Ratan and said: "Here is something for you; I hope it will keep you for some little time." He brought out from his pocket the whole of his month's salary, retaining only a **trifle** for his travelling expenses. Then Ratan fell at his feet and cried: "Oh, Dada, I pray you, don't give me anything, don't in any way trouble about me," and then she ran away out of sight.

35   The postmaster heaved a sigh, took up his carpet bag, put his umbrella over his shoulder, and, accompanied by a man carrying his many-coloured tin trunk, he slowly made for the boat.

36   When he got in and the boat was under way, and the rain-swollen river, like a stream of tears welling up from the earth, swirled and sobbed at her bows, then he felt a pain at heart; the grief-stricken face of a village girl seemed to represent for him the great unspoken pervading grief of Mother Earth herself. At one time he had an impulse to go back, and bring away along with him that lonesome waif, forsaken of the world. But the wind had just filled the sails, the boat had got well into the middle of the turbulent current, and already the village was left behind, and its outlying burning-ground came in sight.

37   So the traveller, borne on the breast of the swift-flowing river, consoled himself with philosophical reflections on the numberless meetings and partings going on in the world—on death, the great parting, from which none returns.

38   But Ratan had no philosophy. She was wandering about the post office in a flood of tears. It may be that she had still a lurking hope in some corner of her heart that her Dada would return, and that is why she could not tear herself away. Alas for our foolish human nature! Its fond mistakes are persistent. The dictates of reason take a long time to assert their own sway. The surest proofs meanwhile are disbelieved. False hope is clung to with all one's might and main, till a day comes when it has sucked the heart dry and it forcibly breaks through its bonds and departs. After that comes the misery of awakening, and then once again the longing to get back into the maze of the same mistakes.

First Read

Read "The Postmaster." After you read, complete the Think Questions below.

☁ THINK QUESTIONS

1. Does the postmaster seem well-adapted to his new home? Use evidence from the text to describe the postmaster's feelings about the village.

2. Based on the text, what can you infer about the life of an orphan in Ulapur? How is Ratan's life in Ulapur different from that of the postmaster? Be sure to cite specific passages from the text.

3. What role does nature, particularly the seasons and the weather, play in the story? Explain how the author uses natural imagery, referring to specific examples from the text in your response.

4. Use context to determine the meaning of the verb **resigned** as it is used in "The Postmaster." Write your definition of *resigned* here and explain how you arrived at it. Use specific examples from the text.

5. The Latin prefix *in-* means "not," and the Latin root "scrutari," means "to search or examine" Using this information and your knowledge of word patterns and relationships, write your best definition of the word **inscrutable** here.

Please note that excerpts and passages in the StudySync® library and this workbook are intended as touchstones to generate interest in an author's work. The excerpts and passages do not substitute for the reading of entire texts, and StudySync® strongly recommends that students seek out and purchase the whole literary or informational work in order to experience it as the author intended. Links to online resellers are available in our digital library. In addition, complete works may be ordered through an authorized reseller by filling out and returning to StudySync® the order form enclosed in this workbook.

Reading & Writing Companion   129

Skill:
Theme

Use the Checklist to analyze Theme in "The Postmaster." Refer to the sample student annotations about Theme in the text.

••• CHECKLIST FOR THEME

In order to identify two or more themes or central ideas of a text, note the following:

✓ the subject and how it relates to the themes in the text

✓ if one or more themes is stated directly in the text

✓ details in the text that help to reveal each theme:

- the title and chapter headings

- details about the setting

- the narrator's or speaker's tone

- characters' thoughts, actions, and dialogue

- the central conflict, climax, and resolution of the conflict

- shifts in characters, setting, or plot events

✓ when and how the themes interact with each other

To determine two or more themes or central ideas of a text and analyze their development over the course of the text, including how they interact and build on one another to produce a complex account, consider the following questions:

✓ What are the themes in the text? When do they emerge?

✓ How does each theme develop over the course of the text?

✓ How do the themes interact and build on one another?

Skill:
Theme

Reread paragraphs 23–32 from "The Postmaster." Then, using the Checklist on the previous page, answer the multiple-choice questions below.

⟳ YOUR TURN

1. This question has two parts. First, answer Part A. Then, answer Part B.

   Part A: Details about the setting in paragraph 27 help develop the theme of disconnection by—

   ○ A. introducing the idea that the postmaster wants to go home.

   ○ B. explaining why Ratan thinks the postmaster will come back.

   ○ C. suggesting that the postmaster will be unhappy no matter where he lives.

   ○ D. emphasizing how quiet and lonely the postmaster's home is.

   Part B: Which of the following quotes from the text BEST supports the answer in Part A?

   ○ A. "... his application for a transfer had been rejected ..."

   ○ B. "... he had resigned his post and was going home."

   ○ C. "... neither of them spoke another word."

   ○ D. "... the thatch water dripped steadily into an earthen vessel ..."

2. The characterization of the postmaster in paragraph 29 contributes to the theme of isolation from others by—

   ○ A. showing he has a sense of humor and can laugh at himself.

   ○ B. suggesting he thinks Ratan is part of the village life he is eager to leave.

   ○ C. explaining why he thinks Ratan's idea is absurd.

   ○ D. introducing the idea that Ratan would not like living in Calcutta.

3. The depiction of the postmaster in paragraphs 31–32 further develops the theme of isolation from others because they—

○ A. demonstrate how frequently he scolds Ratan.

○ B. illustrate his disconnect from the rituals of the villages as well as Ratan's feelings.

○ C. indicate that he is demanding about routines in the morning.

○ D. show that he cares about Ratan's work with the new postmaster.

Skill:
Story Elements

Use the Checklist to analyze Story Elements in "The Postmaster." Refer to the sample student annotations about Story Elements in the text.

••• CHECKLIST FOR STORY ELEMENTS

In order to identify the impact of the author's choices regarding how to develop and relate elements of a story or drama, note the following:

✓ where and when the story takes place, who the main characters are, and the main conflict, or problem, in the plot

✓ the order of the action

✓ how the characters are introduced and developed

✓ the impact that the author's choice of setting has on the characters and their attempt to solve the problem

✓ the point of view the author uses, and how this shapes what readers know about the characters in the story

To analyze the impact of the author's choices regarding how to develop and relate elements of a story or drama, consider the following questions:

✓ How does the author's choices affect the story elements? The development of the plot?

✓ How does the setting influence the characters?

✓ Which elements of the setting impact the plot, and in particular the problem the characters face and must solve?

✓ Are there any flashbacks or other story elements that have an effect on the development of events in the plot? How does the author's choice of utilizing a flashback affect this development?

✓ How does the author introduce and develop characters in the story? Why do you think they made these choices?

Skill:
Story Elements

Reread paragraphs 18 and 19 from "The Postmaster." Then, using the Checklist on the previous page, answer the multiple-choice questions below.

⟳ YOUR TURN

1. How does the economic setting affect the characterization of Ratan in this scene?

   ○ A. It suggests that Ratan has nothing better to do than care for the postmaster.
   ○ B. It hints that the postmaster should pay Ratan for the many services she provides.
   ○ C. It highlights the postmaster's position as an authority figure to Ratan.
   ○ D. It shows that women, even young ones like Ratan, were expected to care for men.

2. The setting of this scene affects the impact of the development of the plot by—

   ○ A. including a flashback to a conflict between the postmaster and his family.
   ○ B. introducing the inner conflict Ratan is experiencing about her role in the postmaster's life.
   ○ C. heightening the growing tension in the story through the depiction of the weather.
   ○ D. showing the climax of the story as the postmaster struggles to rely on Ratan for help.

3. Which statement best evaluates the way the author uses details about the economic context of the story to develop the theme in this scene?

   ○ A. The use of the word *Dada* clearly shows that the orphan Ratan has come to rely on the postmaster as much as he has come to rely on her, which suggests a theme of family.
   ○ B. The postmaster's inability to go to work in a tough economic climate due to sickness strongly develops themes of life's unfairness.
   ○ C. The doctor's visit clearly highlights that other men in the town are of a higher status than the postmaster, which introduces themes of jealousy.
   ○ D. Ratan's eagerness to take on a parental role to the postmaster strongly develops a theme relating to money and power.

Skill:
Summarizing

Use the Checklist to analyze Summarizing in "The Postmaster." Refer to the sample student annotations about Summarizing in the text.

••• CHECKLIST FOR SUMMARIZING

In order to provide an objective summary of a text, note the following:

- ✓ answers to the basic questions *who, what, where, when, why,* and *how*

- ✓ in literature or nonfiction, note how two or more themes or central ideas are developed over the course of the text, and how they interact and build on one another to produce a complex account

- ✓ stay objective, and do not add your own personal thoughts, judgments, or opinions to the summary

To provide an objective summary of a text, consider the following questions:

- ✓ What are the answers to basic *who, what, where, when, why,* and *how* questions in literature and works of nonfiction?

- ✓ Does my summary include how two or more themes or central ideas are developed over the course of the text, and how they interact and build on one another in my summary?

- ✓ Is my summary objective, or have I added my own thoughts, judgments, and personal opinions?

Please note that excerpts and passages in the StudySync® library and this workbook are intended as touchstones to generate interest in an author's work. The excerpts and passages do not substitute for the reading of entire texts, and StudySync® strongly recommends that students seek out and purchase the whole literary or informational work in order to experience it as the author intended. Links to online resellers are available in our digital library. In addition, complete works may be ordered through an authorized reseller by filling out and returning to StudySync® the order form enclosed in this workbook.

Reading & Writing
Companion

135

Skill:
Summarizing

Reread paragraphs 19–25 from the text. Then, using the Checklist on the previous page, answer the multiple-choice questions below.

↻ YOUR TURN

1. What is the most important idea in paragraph 21?

    ○ A. Decisions are a result of both our inner feelings and reality.

    ○ B. Being lonely causes illness.

    ○ C. Resettling in a new place can cause depression and be grueling on the body.

    ○ D. People make poor decisions when they are sick.

2. Which of the following selections best identifies two themes present in the section of text?

    ○ A. "At the voice of her master, she ran up breathlessly, saying: "Were you calling me, Dada?"

    ○ B. "While Ratan was awaiting her call, the postmaster was awaiting a reply to his application."

    ○ C. "Relieved from her duties as nurse, Ratan again took up her old place outside the door. But she no longer heard the same old call."

    ○ D. "In the loneliness of his exile, and in the gloom of the rains, his ailing body needed a little tender nursing."

3. Which statement below is an objective summary of the text?

    ○ A. The postmaster feels bored and lonely in the new village.

    ○ B. Ratan provides the postmaster with some comfort, but this does not cause him to stay.

    ○ C. The postmaster longs for life in Calcutta and this desire to belong outweighs a perceived obligation to Ratan or his post.

    ○ D. The postmaster's sudden departure is selfish and provides little comfort to Ratan.

Close Read

Reread "The Postmaster." As you reread, complete the Skills Focus questions below. Then use your answers and annotations from the questions to help you complete the Write activity.

◎ SKILLS FOCUS

1. In the first four paragraphs, find descriptions of setting—namely, the village of Ulapur and the city of Calcutta. Explain how these descriptions help characterize the postmaster.

2. In paragraphs 1-12, highlight details that show what kind of people the postmaster and Ratan are. How does the narrator want you to feel about each character based on the descriptions he uses in the story? In your annotations, explain how the author's use of language develops the story's themes.

3. Highlight details that show the economic context of the story. Explain how much the characters' wealth, or lack of it, reveals their true character.

4. Highlight elements in "The Postmaster" which answer its basic who, what, where, when, why and how questions. In an annotation, write a brief, objective summary of the text, being sure to note at least two themes developed throughout the text.

5. The last paragraph directly states some themes of the story, particularly as it pertains to the ways circumstances can inform the choices people make. Highlight and restate these themes in your own words, noting how they build on one another. How do the postmaster and Ratan illustrate these themes? How do they reveal their true selves through the decisions they make?

✏ WRITE

COMPARE AND CONTRAST: Write a response comparing and contrasting the postmaster and Ratan's relationship with the village. How do their connections to place impact the story and reveal the text's themes? Be sure to use both evidence from the text and your own original **commentary** to support your analysis.

Please note that excerpts and passages in the StudySync® library and this workbook are intended as touchstones to generate interest in an author's work. The excerpts and passages do not substitute for the reading of entire texts, and StudySync® strongly recommends that students seek out and purchase the whole literary or informational work in order to experience it as the author intended. Links to online resellers are available in our digital library. In addition, complete works may be ordered through an authorized reseller by filling out and returning to StudySync® the order form enclosed in this workbook.

Reading & Writing Companion   137

A Letter to NFL GMs

ARGUMENTATIVE TEXT
Shaquem Griffin
2018

Introduction

Time and time again, Shaquem Griffin (b. 1995) has been told that he doesn't have what it takes to play the punishing game of football. In this open letter to the general managers of the National Football League, Griffin opens up about how he's fought against adversity ever since a congenital illness prevented his left hand from fully developing. From the trash-talk of other players to the humiliation of being ignored by teams and coaches alike, Griffin traces how his life's setbacks have helped to define and strengthen his character. Several weeks after the publication of this letter, Shaquem Griffin was selected in the fifth round of the 2018 NFL Draft by the Seattle Seahawks.

"Nobody was ever going to tell me that I couldn't be great."

Dear NFL GMs,

1   Everything you need to know about me you can learn by going back to when I was eight years old.

2   So let me take you there.

3   It was a Friday night in St. Petersburg, Florida, and I was sleeping — or at least I was trying to. My mind was going crazy because my twin brother, Shaquill, and I had a football game the next morning. He was in the room with me, and he couldn't sleep either, because if we won the next day, we'd be in the playoffs. I had my covers pulled up over my royal blue home jersey — that's right, I was *sleeping* in it. When I was a kid, I always slept in my football jersey the night before a game. That's how ready I was to play every Saturday.

4   So the next morning, when we got to the field — since it was youth football and there were weight **restrictions** — we had to weigh in. And I don't know if they still do it this way, but back then, each coach would weight the opposing team's players, and if you were too heavy or too light, you weren't eligible to play. I had to drop a couple of pounds to make weight for that game, and I had weighed myself the night before and again that morning, so I knew I was good to go.

5   But when the opposing coach weighed me, he said I was too heavy.

6   He told me I couldn't play.

7   So I was heartbroken, right? I mean, I was *devastated*. My coach put his arm around me, told me everything was gonna be O.K. and took me back into our locker room and weighed me himself.

8   This time, I was *not* overweight.

Please note that excerpts and passages in the StudySync® library and this workbook are intended as touchstones to generate interest in an author's work. The excerpts and passages do not substitute for the reading of entire texts, and StudySync® strongly recommends that students seek out and purchase the whole literary or informational work in order to experience it as the author intended. Links to online resellers are available in our digital library. In addition, complete works may be ordered through an authorized reseller by filling out and returning to StudySync® the order form enclosed in this workbook.

Reading & Writing Companion   **139**

9   I was thinking the other coach's scale must be broken or something. It didn't even occur to me that somebody might **deliberately** try to keep me off the football field. I was just a little kid, you know? Too young to understand that people got motives.

10 So my coach took me back over to the guy who weighed me in so we could do it again, and — now, this is a long time ago, so I don't remember exactly what was said, but basically, the opposing coach said that it wasn't about my weight.

11 It was about my *hand*.

12 He said I shouldn't have been allowed to play football *at all*.

13 Because football is for two-handed players.

14 Mind you, I didn't even know this guy. So I didn't know why he had a problem with me playing. I had been playing for a few years and I was pretty good, so maybe he just wanted to keep one of our team's better players off the field so his team had a better chance to win. I honestly don't know.

15 But this was the first time I ever had to deal with somebody telling me I shouldn't — or couldn't — do something because of my hand. Like I was defective or something. Like I didn't belong.

16 And that was the moment I realized I was always going to have to prove people wrong.

. . .

17 I'm not going to get into an explanation of the condition I was born with that prevented the fingers of my left hand from fully developing. Or talk about the

time when I was four years old and I tried to cut my own fingers off with a kitchen knife because I was in constant pain. Or about when I got my left hand amputated shortly after. That's stuff you probably already know about anyway — and if you don't, you can Google it. The story is out there. And it's not some sob story or anything like that. It's not even a sad story — at least not to me.

18   It's just . . . *my* story.

19   I'm blessed to have thick skin. But I'm even more blessed to have a family that never let me make excuses and who raised me to never listen to anybody who told me I couldn't do something — especially because of my hand.

20   My dad used to build all kinds of **contraptions** to help me lift weights. We had this one thing   we called it "the book," and it was basically a piece of wood wrapped up in some cloth that I would hold up against the bar with my left arm when I bench pressed so my arms would be even. We had another block that I used for stuff like dips and push-ups, and I had chains and other straps to hold dumbbells for things like curls and shrugs.

21   And my dad used to work me, Shaquill and our older brother, Andre, hard.

22   In our backyard, we had a couple of stacks of cinder blocks with a stick across the top, like a hurdle. And when we would run routes, we would have to jump over the hurdle and do other obstacles mid-route. Then my dad would throw us the ball, and he'd throw it *hard*, right at our chest. And every time we dropped it, he would say, "Nothing comes easy."

23   That was kind of his motto — not just for me, but for all of us.

24   *Nothing comes easy.*

25   Man . . . I hated those workouts. There were definitely times when I wanted to quit. Sometimes, when my dad threw the ball so hard that it bounced off my chest or it hit me in the face, I would be like, "I don't wanna do this anymore."

26   But he never let me quit.

27   "You'll thank me one day," he'd say.

28   At the time, I didn't believe him. Now, I understand, and I thank him every chance I get, because all that work in the backyard helped me to develop the mentality that I can handle anything — that whatever you come at me with, I can come back at you even harder.

29   That's what I did that day when that youth coach told me I shouldn't be playing football.

30　I ended up being allowed to play that day, and I remember it like it was yesterday. It was near the end of the game, and we were ahead. I was on defense, playing linebacker. The outside receiver ran a slant route, and I read the play, jumped the route, dove in the air and caught the ball, flipping over onto my back to secure it before I hit the ground. It was the first time I had ever intercepted a pass in a game, and it basically sealed the win for us and sent us to the playoffs.

31　I got up and ran off the field, holding the ball up in the air with my one good hand and thinking that from that moment forward, nobody was ever going to tell me that I didn't belong on a football field.

32　And nobody was ever going to tell me that I couldn't be great.

33　I rode that mentality all the way through high school.

34　I got picked on because of my hand and I had guys trash-talk me and stuff like that, but most of the time, I just ignored it. On the football field, I got off to kind of a slow start adjusting to the high school game, but eventually I grew to be a leader and a team captain.

35　But right here, instead of talking about the success I've had, I think I would rather tell you about some of the more difficult times in my life — the lowest points. Because I think that's when true character shows. That's when you find out who people really are — what they're really made of.

36　And the lowest points for me came when I was in college.

37　I went to UCF thinking I was going to play as a freshman, and everybody was going to know my name. I was so confident.

38　But it wasn't like that at all.

39　My freshman year, I got redshirted[1]. The following year, I played well in the spring and worked my way up to second string on the depth chart.

---

1. **redshirted** in college athletics, being "redshirted" means having one's participation delayed or suspended in order to increase the length of eligibility for the program

40 Then, right before the season-opener against Penn State, I got bumped down to third string.

41 The next week, I got moved to the scout team.

42 And nobody told me why.

43 Whenever I asked one of the coaches why I was being demoted, they just said things like, "Keep working," and, "Stay focused," and, "Your time will come."

44 So that's basically what I did for my first three years at UCF.

45 I think the hardest part about those first few years was watching Shaquill play on Saturdays. We've always told each other since we were kids that no matter what either of us is doing, we live through each other. His success is my success, and vice versa. And we meant that.

46 I didn't travel with the team much those first few years. When it came time for the team to go on the road, my brother and our two roommates, who were also on the team, all went. So on Saturdays, it was just me, alone in our dorm[2] room watching the game. Sometimes the game wasn't even on ESPN or FOX or anything, so I had to stream it on my laptop. I'd be sitting there on the couch, alone, the whole dorm silent except for the game commentary as I was watching my brother play . . . and living through him.

47 I used to tell my mom all the time that college was a negative place for me. Not UCF in general — I love my school and I'll represent it forever. It was just . . . that dorm room, man.

Unit 412, Room C.

48 I spent so much time those first three years in Orlando sitting in that room, wondering why I wasn't getting an opportunity to play on Saturdays. It got to

2. **dorm** short for dormitory, a facility where college students live

NOTES

the point where that dorm was just so full of negative **vibes**, because I pretty much kept everything to myself. I didn't really talk to anybody about what I was feeling — especially not to Shaquill.

49 It's a tough spot to be in, right? I mean, my twin brother was doing his thing. The dream was happening for him, and he was earning every single bit of it, working hard and showing out on the field.

50 I wanted that for myself so badly, and even though I felt like I was good enough, and I was doing everything my coaches asked me to, I wasn't even getting an opportunity. And the last thing I wanted to do was dump all my negativity on Shaquill and bring him down. So I made sure I was always positive around him. I never talked to him about how I was feeling those first three years.

51 The lowest of the lows was probably the summer before my third season, when the coaches had most of the guys stay in Orlando to work out while other guys went home for the summer.

52 They kept Shaquill at UCF for the summer.

53 They sent me home to St. Petersburg.

54 It was the first time Shaquill and I had ever really been apart.

55 I spent that summer working with my dad and Andre. My dad has a tow truck, so I would wake up at 7 a.m. and go to work with him, towing cars. I would get off around 6 p.m. and go to my old high school to work out with the track team, then I'd meet up with Andre around 8 p.m. and work with him until midnight, cleaning offices at the local Chevy dealership.

56 I did that every day, Monday through Saturday, for the entire summer.

57 I remember one time, when I was working with my dad, we towed this one guy's car, and when we dropped it off, the guy pulled a five-dollar bill out of his pocket and went to hand it to me. But before I took it, he pulled it back and ripped it in half. He gave me one half and put the other half back in his pocket. I didn't know if I was supposed to laugh or if I should have been mad. I just kind of looked at the guy.

58 He looked back at me and said, "Keep on working, son. Because nothing comes easy."

59 I still have that ripped-up five-dollar bill somewhere at my parents' house because I never want to forget what that guy said to me that day — it was the same thing my dad always used to say when I was a kid.

NOTES

60   *Nothing comes easy.*

61   And looking back, at the time, I think I needed to be reminded of that. Because if sitting in my dorm room alone and watching games on my laptop was a low point, towing cars and cleaning out trash cans in those office cubicles at night was even worse.

62   Honestly, that summer was the first and only time since I was a little kid jumping hurdles and trying to catch rockets from my dad in the backyard that I thought about quitting football.

63   Those were pretty dark times for me.

64   Then, after I went back to UCF for my third season and we went 0–12, Coach Frost came in and brought me back into the light.

65   You probably know what happened next: Over the next two seasons, Coach Frost turned an 0–12 program into an undefeated, national championship team. (That's right, I said national championship team. And nobody can convince me otherwise.)

66   Along the way, he gave me the opportunity I had been waiting for ever since I first arrived at UCF.

67   And I took advantage of it.

68   I think that what I did on the field, especially this past season, speaks for itself. So I don't feel like I need to get into all that. I'll let the tape do the talking.

69   Besides, I don't define myself by my successes.

70   I define myself by **adversity,** and how I've persevered.

. . .

71   I don't sleep in my jersey the night before games anymore. But I did sleep at the football facility for basically the whole preseason camp this last season. I went out and bought a blow-up mattress and a comforter, and then I went to Publix and stocked up on drinks and snacks and stuff so I had everything I needed. And instead of going back and forth to my dorm during camp, I slept at the football facility and lifted weights and watched extra film at night.

72   I just knew it was going to be my last camp at UCF, so I wanted to get the full experience, you know?

73   I just think that as guys progress through their football careers, they start thinking about the game differently. They start thinking about getting their

Please note that excerpts and passages in the StudySync® library and this workbook are intended as touchstones to generate interest in an author's work. The excerpts and passages do not substitute for the reading of entire texts, and StudySync® strongly recommends that students seek out and purchase the whole literary or informational work in order to experience it as the author intended. Links to online resellers are available in our digital library. In addition, complete works may be ordered through an authorized reseller by filling out and returning to StudySync® the order form enclosed in this workbook.

Reading & Writing Companion   **145**

NOTES

college paid for, or making it to the NFL so they can take care of their families. They start looking at it as a job — and they should, because to excel at the highest levels, you have to take the game seriously. It's a big responsibility.

74 But I think some guys forget about why they started playing back when they were kids — how they loved the game so much that they'd sleep in their jersey the night before a game.

75 I started playing football because I loved it. And yeah, just like anybody else, my view of the game has definitely changed as I've gotten older.

76 But it hasn't turned into a job or an obligation.

77 It's developed into a *purpose*.

78 I've had people doubt me my whole life, and I know that there are a lot of kids out there with various deformities or birth defects or whatever labels people want to put on them, and they're going to be doubted, too. And I'm convinced that God has put me on this earth for a reason, and that reason is to show people that it doesn't matter what anybody else says, because people are going to doubt you **regardless**. That's a fact of life for everybody, but especially for those with birth defects or other so-called disabilities.

79 The important thing is that you don't doubt *yourself*.

80 I feel like all the boys and girls out there with birth defects . . . we have our own little nation, and we've got to support each other, because everybody in this world deserves to show what they can do without anybody telling them they *can't*.

81 I know there are some scouts and coaches — and even some of you GMs out there — who are probably doubting me, and that's O.K. I get it. I only have one hand, and because of that, there have always been people who have questioned whether or not I could play this game.

82 If you're one of those GMs who believes that I can play in the NFL, I just want to say thank you. I appreciate you, and I'm excited for the opportunity to play for you and prove you right.

83 And if one you're of those who is doubting me . . . well, I want to thank you, too. Because you're what keeps me motivated every day to work hard and play even harder.

84 Back when I was eight years old, I played because I loved the game. I still do. But now, I also play because I believe it's my purpose. I know that it won't come easy. Nothing comes easy. But I will fulfill that purpose. I have no doubt.

85   Sincerely,

86   Shaquem Griffin
University of Central Florida
2017 National Champions (13–0)

By Shaquem Griffin, 2018. Used by permission of The Players' Tribune.

✏ WRITE

EXPLANATORY ESSAY: Why do you think Shaquem Griffin chose to write an open letter to general managers in the NFL? What is Griffin's point of view in the letter and how does he use his personal experiences to defend it? What do you think he hoped to accomplish by publishing this letter online? Write a response in which you answer these questions. Remember to use textual evidence to support your response.

Please note that excerpts and passages in the StudySync® library and this workbook are intended as touchstones to generate interest in an author's work. The excerpts and passages do not substitute for the reading of entire texts, and StudySync® strongly recommends that students seek out and purchase the whole literary or informational work in order to experience it as the author intended. Links to online resellers are available in our digital library. In addition, complete works may be ordered through an authorized reseller by filling out and returning to StudySync® the order form enclosed in this workbook.

Reading & Writing
Companion

147

Men We Reaped:
A Memoir

INFORMATIONAL TEXT
Jesmyn Ward
2013

Introduction

Jesmyn Ward (b. 1977) grew up in DeLisle, Mississippi, a small rural town along the Gulf Coast. She was the first woman to win the National Book Award twice: in 2011, for her second novel, *Salvage the Bones*, as well as for her third novel, 2017's *Sing, Unburied, Sing*. Ward's writing primarily focuses on the lives of the people in the communities where she grew up. She is known for creating honest, robust, complicated characters, and for her portrayals of life along the Gulf Coast with all of its lyricism and mystery. *Men We Reaped: A Memoir* traces Ward's search for meaning after her world was turned upside down by the violent deaths of her brother and four close personal friends over a four-year period.

"Somebody died here."

NOTES

Prologue

1   Whenever my mother drove us from coastal Mississippi to New Orleans to visit my father on the weekend, she would say, "Lock the doors." After my mother and father split for the last time before they divorced, my father moved to New Orleans, while we remained in DeLisle, Mississippi.

2   My father's first house in the Crescent City was a modest one-bedroom, painted yellow, with bars on the window. It was in Shrewsbury, a small Black neighborhood that spread under and to the north of the causeway overpass. The house was **bounded** by a fenced industrial yard to the north and by the rushing, plunking sound of the cars on the elevated interstate to the south. I was the oldest of four, and since I was the oldest, I was the one who bossed my one brother, Joshua, and my two sisters, Nerissa and Charine, and my cousin Aldon, who lived with us for years, to arrange my father's extra sheets and sofa cushion into pallets on the living room floor so we all had enough room to sleep. My parents, who were attempting to reconcile and would fail, slept in the only bedroom. Joshua insisted that there was a ghost in the house, and at night we'd lie on our backs in the TV-less living room, watch the barred shadows slink across the walls, and wait for something to change, for something that wasn't supposed to be there, to move.

3   "Somebody died here," Josh said.

4   "How you know?" I said.

5   "Daddy told me," he said.

6   "You just trying to scare us," I said. What I didn't say: *It's working*.

7   I was in junior high then, in the late eighties and early nineties, and I attended a majority White, Episcopalian Mississippi private school. I was a small-town girl, and my classmates in Mississippi were as provincial as I was. My classmates called New Orleans the "murder capital." They told horror stories about White people being shot while unloading groceries from their cars. Gang **initiations**, they said. What was unspoken in this conversation—and,

Copyright © BookheadEd Learning, LLC

NOTES

given the racist proclivities of more than a few of my classmates, I'm surprised that it was unspoken—was that these gangsters, ruthlessly violent and untethered by common human decency, were Black. My school peers would often glance at me when they spoke about Black people. I was a scholarship kid, only attending the school because my mother was a maid for a few wealthy families on the Mississippi coast who sponsored my tuition. For most of my junior high and high school years, I was the only Black girl in the school. Whenever my classmates spoke about Black people or New Orleans and tried to not look at me but inevitably did, I stared back at them and thought about the young men I knew from New Orleans, my father's half brothers.

8   Uncle Bookie was our favorite of my father's half brothers. He and his brothers had spent their lives in the neighborhoods my classmates most feared. Uncle Bookie looked the most like the grandfather I'd barely known, who'd died of a **stroke** at age fifty. He had a chest like a barrel, and his eyes closed when he smiled. On hot days, Uncle Bookie would walk us through Shrewsbury toward the highway in the sky, to a ramshackle shotgun house, maroon in my memory, that stood on the corner. The lady who lived in the house sold ice pops out of the back. They were liquid sugar, and melted too quickly in the heat. On the walk to her yard, he'd crack jokes, gather more kids, lead us over the melting asphalt like a hood pied piper[1]. Once our ice pops melted to syrup in their cardboard cups, once Joshua and I had licked the sugar water from our hands and arms, Uncle Bookie would play games with us in the street: kickball, football, and basketball. He laughed when the football hit one of us in the mouth, leaving it sore and swollen, his eyes slit to the thin side of a penny. On some days he would take us with our father and his pit bull to the park under the highway. There, my father fought his dog against other dogs. The other men who watched or coaxed their dogs to savagery were dark and sweat-glazed as their animals in the heat. My brother and I always stood close to our uncle. We grabbed his forearms, holding tightly, flinching as the cars boomed overhead and the animals ripped at each other. Afterward, the dogs panted and smiled while they bled, and my brother and I relaxed our grip on our uncle, and were happy to leave the shadowed world and the threat of a dog lunging outside the fighting circle.

9   "Daddy ain't tell you no story about nobody dying in here," I said.

10   "Yeah, he did," Joshua said.

11   "You telling it," Aldon said.

12   When I was in high school, I could not reconcile the myth of New Orleans to the reality, but I knew that there was truth somewhere. My father and mother

---

1. **pied piper** a folkloric character who leads people into trouble or calamity by offering false promises

sat in the front seat of the car during those early nineties visits, when they were still married but separated, when they still had the easy rapport that years of marriage engenders, and they talked about shootings, about beatings, about murder. They gave the violence of New Orleans many names. We never saw any of that when we visited my father. But we listened to the chain-link fence rattle in the industrial yard next to my father's house and the night stretched on interminably, and we listened to my brother tell us ghost stories.

13　Yet we knew another New Orleans existed. We saw that when we piled into my mother's car and rode past the red brick projects scattered through New Orleans, two-story buildings with sagging iron balconies, massive old trees standing like sentinels at each side of the buildings, women gesticulating and scratching their heads, small dark children playing angrily, happily, sulking on the broken sidewalks. I eyed the young men through the car window. Men in sagging pants with their heads bent together, murmuring, ducking into corner stores that sold poboys shrimp oyster. I wondered what the men were talking about. I wondered who they were. I wondered what their lives were like. I wondered if they were murderers. At night on my father's living room floor, I asked Joshua again.

14　"What Daddy say happen?" I said.

15　"Said somebody got shot," Joshua said.

16　"What somebody?"

17　"A man," he said to the ceiling. Charine burrowed into my side.

18　"Shut up," Nerissa said. Aldon sighed.

19　When we left my father to go home to DeLisle, as we did every Sunday, I was sad. We all were sad, I think, even my mother, who was trying to make their marriage work, despite the distance and the years of infidelity. She'd even been contemplating moving to New Orleans, a city she hated. I missed my father. I didn't want to return to school in Mississippi on Monday morning, to walk through the glass doors to the large, fluorescent-lit classrooms, the old desks, my classmates perched on the backs of them, wearing collared shirts and khaki shorts, their legs spread, their eyeliner blue. I didn't want them to look at me after saying something about Black people, didn't want to have to avert my eyes so they didn't see me studying them, studying the entitlement they wore like another piece of clothing. Our drive home took us through New Orleans East, across the Isle Sauvage bayou[2], over the gray murmur of Lake Pontchartrain, through the billboards and strip malls of Slidell into

2. **bayou** In parts of the Southern U.S., an area of marshy, slow-moving water connected to a river or lake.

NOTES

Mississippi. We took I-10 past the pine wall of Stennis Space Center, past Bay St. Louis, past Diamondhead to DeLisle. Once there, we would have exited the long, pitted highway, driven past Du Pont, shielded like Stennis behind its wall of pine trees, past the railroad tracks, past the small wooden houses set in small fields and small sandy yards, trees setting the porches in shade. Here horses stood still in fields, munching grass, seeking cool. Goats chewed fence posts.

20 DeLisle and Pass Christian, the two towns where all of my family hails from, are not New Orleans. Pass Christian squats beside the man-made beach of the Gulf of Mexico alongside Long Beach, the Bay of St. Louis at its back, while DeLisle hugs the back of the Bay of St. Louis before spreading away and thinning further upcountry. The streets of both towns are sleepy through much of the barely bearable summer, and through much of the winter, when temperatures hover near freezing. In DeLisle during the summers, there are sometimes crowds on Sundays at the county park because younger people come out to play basketball and play music from their cars. In the spring, the older people gather at the local baseball field, where Negro leagues from throughout the South come to play. On Halloween, children still walk or ride on the backs of pickup trucks through the neighborhood from house to house to trick-or-treat. On All Saints Day[3], families gather around loved ones' graves, bring nylon and canvas folding chairs to sit in after they've cleaned headstones and sandy plots, arranged potted mums, and shared food. They talk into the evening, burn fires, wave away the last of the fall gnats. This is not a murder capital.

21 Most of the Black families in DeLisle have lived there as far back as they can remember, including mine, in houses many of them built themselves. These houses, small shotguns and A-frames, were built in waves, the oldest in the thirties by our great-grandparents, the next in the fifties by our grandparents, the next in the seventies and eighties by our parents, who used contractors. These modest houses, ours included, had two to three bedrooms with gravel and dirt driveways and rabbit hutches and scupadine vineyards in the back. Poor and working-class, but proud. There is no public housing at all in DeLisle, and the project housing that existed before Hurricane Katrina in Pass Christian consisted of several small redbrick duplexes and a few subdivisions with single-family homes, which housed some Black people, some Vietnamese. Now, seven years after Katrina, developers build two- and three-bedroom houses up on fifteen- to twenty-foot stilts where this public housing stood, and these houses fill quickly with those still displaced from the storm, or young adults from Pass Christian and DeLisle who want to live in their hometown. Hurricane Katrina made that impossible for several years, since it

---

3. **All Saints Day** in Western Christianity, a celebration that immediately follows All Hallows' Eve (Halloween)

NOTES

razed most of the housing in Pass Christian, and decimated what was closest to the bayou in DeLisle. Coming home to DeLisle as an adult has been harder for this reason, a concrete one. And then there are abstract reasons, too.

22 As Joshua said when we were kids hunting down ghosts: Somebody died here. From 2000 to 2004, five Black young men I grew up with died, all violently, in seemingly unrelated deaths. The first was my brother, Joshua, in October 2000. The second was Ronald in December 2002. The third was C. J. in January 2004. The fourth was Demond in February 2004. The last was Roger in June 2004. That's a brutal list, in its immediacy and its **relentlessness**, and it's a list that silences people. It silenced me for a long time. To say this is difficult is understatement; telling this story is the hardest thing I've ever done. But my ghosts were once people, and I cannot forget that. I cannot forget that when I am walking the streets of DeLisle, streets that seem even barer since Katrina. Streets that seem even more empty since all these deaths, where instead of hearing my friends or my brother playing music from their cars at the county park, the only sound I hear is a tortured parrot that one of my cousins owns, a parrot that screams so loudly it sounds through the neighborhood, a scream like a wounded child, from a cage so small the parrot's crest barely clears the top of the cage while its tail brushes the bottom. Sometimes when that parrot screams, sounding its rage and grief, I wonder at my neighborhood's silence. I wonder why silence is the sound of our subsumed rage, our accumulated grief. I decide this is not right, that I must give voice to this story. I'm telling you: there's a ghost in here, Joshua said. Because this is my story just as it is the story of those lost young men, and because this is my family's story just as it is my community's story, it is not straightforward. To tell it, I must tell the story of my town, and the history of my community. And then I must revisit each of the five young black men who died: follow them backward in time, from Rog's death to Demond's death to C. J.'s death to Ronald's death to my brother's death. At the same time, I must tell this story forward through time, so between those chapters where my friends and my brother live and speak and breathe again for a few paltry pages, I must write about my family and how I grew up. My hope is that learning something about our lives and the lives of the people in my community will mean that when I get to the heart, when my marches forward through the past and backward from the present meet in the middle with my brother's death, I'll understand a bit better why this epidemic happened, about how the history of racism and economic inequality and lapsed public and personal responsibility festered and turned sour and spread here. Hopefully, I'll understand why my brother died while I live, and why I've been saddled with this rotten story.

© Jesmyn Ward, 2013, *Men We Reaped*, Bloomsbury Publishing, Inc.

WRITE

LITERARY ANALYSIS: This excerpt contains descriptions of multiple settings that were significant in the author's life. Write a response in which you evaluate how the social and economic context of the settings influences the characterization and plot. Remember to use textual evidence to support your response.

Extended Writing Project and Grammar

EXTENDED
WRITING
PROJECT
NARRATIVE
WRITING

Narrative Writing Process: Plan

| PLAN | DRAFT | REVISE | EDIT AND PUBLISH |

Great leaders the world over have emerged from troubled times to champion causes and to safeguard the lives of others. In fiction, the same is true: the worst of times may make a hero from a most unassuming character. This is evident in narratives that reach into the past, those that grapple with the circumstances of today, and those that look to the future here on Earth or among the stars.

WRITING PROMPT

How do leaders rise up and guide others?

Select an issue in today's society that is causing conflict in your own life or among groups of people. Write a personal or fictional narrative about this conflict. If you are writing a personal narrative, explain how this conflict has affected your life or the lives of your friends or family. Then, describe how you or someone in your life has demonstrated leadership skills in response to this conflict. If you are writing a fictional narrative, create a fictional character who belongs to one of the groups involved in this conflict and develop a plot outline set in the present or near future in which this character moves from being a passive member to a powerful leader of the group. Using that outline, write a narrative that shows this character's transformation and the effect this transformation has on the conflict. Be sure your narrative includes the following:

- a plot with a beginning, middle, and end
- a clear setting
- characters and dialogue
- a distinct conflict and resolution
- a clear theme

Introduction to Narrative Writing

Narrative writing tells a story of experiences or events that have been imagined by a writer or that have happened in real life. Good narrative writing effectively uses genre characteristics and craft such as relevant descriptive details and a purposeful structure with a series of events that includes a beginning, middle, and end. The characteristics of narrative writing include:

- setting
- characters

- plot
- theme

- point of view

In addition to these characteristics, narrative writers carefully craft their work through their use of dialogue, details, word choice, and figurative language. These choices help to shape the tone, mood, and overall style of the text. Effective narratives combine these genre characteristics and craft to engage the reader.

As you continue with this Extended Writing Project, you'll receive more instruction and practice in crafting each of the characteristics of narrative writing to create your own narrative.

Before you get started on your own personal or fictional narrative, read this narrative that one student, Isaiah, wrote in response to the writing prompt. As you read the Model, highlight and annotate the features of narrative writing that Isaiah included in his narrative.

☰ STUDENT MODEL

Daisy's Hero

1 David stood next to the hospital bed. The thick shade on the window kept out the sunshine, so the room was dim and cold. The sour smell of cleaning supplies and sickness burned his nostrils. The steady beep of the heart monitor was interrupted only by his parents' whispers. David watched as Daisy slept. The same question played on an endless loop in his head. How did this happen again? Daisy was 11 years old now. The cancer had been gone for seven years. David had studied the topic in his honors biology class, so he understood how cancer cells are formed and spread. Still, as he looked down at his little sister, he couldn't understand how the leukemia could come back after all this time.

2 Lost in his thoughts, David caught only bits of information from his parents' conversation with the doctor. The bad news hovered in the air like an angry wasp, and David hoped that by keeping still and quiet, he could trick it into flying away and leaving his family alone. He caught the words "aggressive" and "experimental treatment." The cancer was worse this time. It was stronger and more resistant to treatment. David wrapped his hand around Daisy's wrist. She had never seemed smaller. He closed his eyes and wished for a miracle. He had never wished more fervently for anything in his life, not even that time he almost won tickets to the World Series.

3 When Daisy came home from the hospital, the family had already made some changes. David helped turn their home office into a bedroom. The hospital bed they rented looked intimidating next to the old wooden desk and bookcases, so David lovingly filled the room with Daisy's stuffed animals. His mom left her bookkeeping job since Daisy couldn't go to school anymore. His dad started working a second job at a 24-hour supermarket to make up for the lost income. The medical bills overflowed their mailbox, and money grew

tight. David tried to keep a positive attitude, but every time he heard Daisy wheeze, "I'm just so tired," his outlook grew a little more bleak.

4   On one blustery February morning, it became clear to David that the family was in trouble.

5   David was alone in his room when his dad came through the door. "Son, I'm afraid I have some bad news," he began.

6   David's heart rate shot up immediately. "About Daisy?" he blurted. "Is she okay?"

7   His father offered a weak smile. "Your sister is okay. This has nothing to do with her. Your mother and I were up all night crunching the numbers, and we just don't have the money for your spring training trip and new uniform this year. I'm sorry."

8   That meant he couldn't play baseball this season, his last in high school. David knew that the family needed to make sacrifices for Daisy, but he couldn't help but feel angry that he had to give up the one thing he truly loved. David quickly turned away to hide his face. He wanted to shout that this wasn't fair. Hadn't their life changed enough? Didn't they understand that he needed this final season with his team? Was it too much to ask for something for himself for once?

9   "It's okay," he exhaled as his father left the room.

10 A month later, as David and his mother were driving home from school, they heard a loud bang and the car came to a stop in the middle of the road. After an expensive emergency tow and a mechanic's inspection, they learned that the engine would need to be replaced. The estimate was more than $2000. It was the family's only car. With Daisy's medical bills, they couldn't afford to spend that kind of money on repairs. But without the car, they couldn't take Daisy to get her cancer treatments. David's guilt over feeling upset about baseball was immediate and crushing. He was wrong to be selfish when his family was counting on him to be strong. He gently placed his arm around his mother's shoulders and gave her a tight squeeze.

11 "It'll be okay, Mom," he said brightly. "I swear."

12 Now he just had to find a way to keep that promise.

13 David had been avoiding his baseball teammates since his unexpected retirement. Stories about preseason practices kept him away from their lunch tables, and it was painful to watch them head off to the field after school. But after three years of playing together, his former teammates were still his best friends and the only people he knew he could count on for help.

14 The locker room looked the same as it had the last time David entered it. The harsh overhead lights reflected off the red metal lockers, and the floor was just as mysteriously damp as it had always been. He took careful and deliberate steps, pausing only for a moment to glance at the locker that should have been his. His coach was the first to spot him.

15 "David!" Coach Warner boomed. "I hope this means you're coming back to the team."

16 "Not quite, Coach," David could feel everyone staring at him. Suddenly shy, he lowered his voice and asked, "Can we talk in your office for a minute?"

17 When David and Coach Warner emerged from the office a few minutes later, they had a plan. The team would host a fundraiser for David's family. Now all they needed were volunteers. Coach had barely finished his speech before every team member's hand was in the air. David beamed.

18 The fundraiser was a success. The team raised enough money to pay for the car repairs with a bit left over to cover some of Daisy's medical bills. That night at the dinner table, David's dad clapped him on the back and said, "You saved the day, son. How does it feel to be a hero?"

19 David flashed a smile as he thought about everything that had happened. "Don't be silly, Dad. I'm no hero. But I think I figured out what I want to do with my spare time now that I'm not playing baseball. I found a local organization that helps families who are dealing with childhood cancers, and I volunteered to help. I'm going to lead the team on a new fundraiser for another family. Coach says he'll help me do a new one next year when I'm home from college for spring break."

20 Daisy reached up from her wheelchair and grabbed David's hand. "Say whatever you want, big brother, but you'll always be my hero."

✎ WRITE

Writers often take notes about story ideas before they sit down to write. Think about what you've learned so far about organizing narrative writing to help you begin prewriting.

- **Purpose:** What issue do you want to write about, and why is it a problem?

- **Audience:** Who is your audience, and what message do you want to express to your audience?

- **Setting:** Where and when will your story be set? What kinds of problems might the characters face? How might the setting of your story affect the characters and problem?

- **Characters:** What types of characters would you like to write about in your narrative?

- **Plot:** What events will lead to the resolution of the conflict while keeping a reader engaged?

- **Theme/Reflection:** If you are writing an imagined narrative, what general message about life do you want to express? If you are writing a real narrative, what careful thoughts about the significance of your experience will you include?

- **Point of View:** From which point of view should your story be told, and why?

Response Instructions

Use the questions in the bulleted list to write a one-paragraph summary. Your summary should describe what will happen in your narrative.

Don't worry about including all of the details now; focus only on the most essential and important elements. You will refer to this short summary as you continue through the steps of the writing process.

Please note that excerpts and passages in the StudySync® library and this workbook are intended as touchstones to generate interest in an author's work. The excerpts and passages do not substitute for the reading of entire texts, and StudySync® strongly recommends that students seek out and purchase the whole literary or informational work in order to experience it as the author intended. Links to online resellers are available in our digital library. In addition, complete works may be ordered through an authorized reseller by filling out and returning to StudySync® the order form enclosed in this workbook.

Reading & Writing Companion   161

ORGANIZING
NARRATIVE WRITING

sync·skills

Skill:
Organizing Narrative Writing

As you consider how to organize your writing for your narrative, use the following questions as a guide:

- Who is the narrator, and who are the characters in the story?

- Will the story be told from one or multiple points of view?

- Where will the story take place?

- Have I created a problem that characters will have to face and resolve, while noting its significance to the characters?

- Have I created a smooth progression of experiences or plot events, building toward a particular outcome?

Here are some strategies to help you create a smooth progression of experiences or events in your narrative:

- Establish a context

  > choose a setting and a problem that characters will have to face and resolve, noting its significance to the characters

  > decide how the conflict will be resolved

    o the problem often builds to a climax, when the characters are forced to take action

- Introduce a narrator and/or characters

  > characters can be introduced all at once or over the course of the narrative

  > choose the role each character will play in the story

  > choose one or multiple points of view, either first or third person

    o a first-person narrator can be a participant or character in the story

    o a third-person narrator tells the story as an outside observer

⟳ YOUR TURN

While identifying the problem that his characters will need to face in his narrative, Isaiah writes, "The main character's sister is very sick. He is sad." How would you change this statement of the problem to involve more characters? Choose the best revision of the statement.

○ A. The main character's sister has cancer, and the medical bills require the family to make sacrifices.

○ B. The main character's sister has cancer, and he is in denial and considers running away.

○ C. The main character's sister has cancer, and she spends most of her time in the hospital.

○ D. The main character's sister has cancer, and he doesn't know how to help her.

⟳ YOUR TURN

Complete the chart below by writing a short summary of what will happen in each section of your narrative.

Narrative Sequence	Event
Exposition	
Rising Action	
Climax	
Falling Action	
Resolution	

Please note that excerpts and passages in the StudySync® library and this workbook are intended as touchstones to generate interest in an author's work. The excerpts and passages do not substitute for the reading of entire texts, and StudySync® strongly recommends that students seek out and purchase the whole literary or informational work in order to experience it as the author intended. Links to online resellers are available in our digital library. In addition, complete works may be ordered through an authorized reseller by filling out and returning to StudySync® the order form enclosed in this workbook.

Reading & Writing Companion   163

Narrative Writing Process: Draft

| PLAN | DRAFT | REVISE | EDIT AND PUBLISH |

You have already made progress toward writing your narrative. Now it is time to draft your narrative.

✎ WRITE

Use your plan and other responses in your Binder to draft your narrative. You may also have new ideas as you begin drafting. Feel free to explore those new ideas as you have them. You can also ask yourself these questions to ensure that your writing is focused, organized, and detailed:

Draft Checklist:

☐ **Purpose and Focus:** Have I made my conflict clear to readers? Have I included only relevant information and nothing extraneous that might confuse my readers?

☐ **Organization:** Does the sequence of events in my story make sense? Will readers be engaged by the organization and want to keep reading to find out what happens next?

☐ **Ideas and Details:** Does my writing include engaging ideas and details? Will my readers be able to easily understand descriptions of characters, settings, or events?

Before you submit your draft, read it over carefully. You want to be sure that you've responded to all aspects of the prompt.

Here is Isaiah's fictional narrative. As you read, notice how Isaiah develops his draft to be focused, organized, and detailed. As he continues to revise and edit his narrative, he will find and improve weak spots in his writing, as well as correct any language or punctuation mistakes.

☰ STUDENT MODEL: FIRST DRAFT

~~David stood next to the hospital bed and watch as Daisy slept. The same question play on a loop in his head, how did this happen again? Daisy was 11 years old now. The cancer had been gone for seven years. David had been studied the topic in its honors biology class, so he understood how cancer cells work. Still, as he looked down at her little sister, he couldn't understand how the lukeamia could come back after all this time.~~

David stood next to the hospital bed. The thick shade on the window kept out the sunshine, so the room was dim and cold. The sour smell of cleaning supplies and sickness burned his nostrils. The steady beep of the heart monitor was interrupted only by his parents' whispers. David watched as Daisy slept. The same question played on an endless loop in his head. How did this happen again? Daisy was 11 years old now. The cancer had been gone for seven years. David had studied the topic in his honors biology class, so he understood how cancer cells are formed and spread. Still, as he looked down at his little sister, he couldn't understand how the leukemia could come back after all this time.

The bad news was a shock. The cancer was worse this time. It was strongest and more resistent to treatment. David held her sister's hand. She had never seemed small. He wished for a miracle.

David helped turn their home office into a bedroom. He helped his mom organize her room. His dad started working a second job at a 24-hour supermarket to make up for the lost income. Money grew tight. David did his best to stay optimistic, but each time he looked at his sister, he grew more afraid.

~~One morning, it became clearly to David that the family was in trouble.~~

~~"I'm afraid I have some bad news," he began.~~

 Skill:
Story Beginnings

Isaiah decides to create a more engaging beginning. He wants readers to feel as if they are in the hospital with David. So he adds sight, smell, and sound details to help readers visualize the scene and connect with David.

David felt scared. Bad news was probably about Daisy. She had been going to get cancer treatments for a while now, it had been working. He wanted to hear only good news about it.

"About Daisy?" he asked. "Is she okay?"

His father offers a week smile. "Your sister is okay. This has nothing to do with it. Your mother and I were up all night crunching the numbers, and we just don't have the money for your spring training trip and new uniform this year. I'm sorry."

David quick turned away to hide his face. He wanted to shout that this wasn't fair. Hadn't our life changed enough? Didn't he understand that he needed this final season with his team? Was it too much to ask for something for himself for once.

"It's okay," he said as their father left the room.

On one blustery February morning, it became clear to David that the family was in trouble.

David was alone in his room when his dad came through the door. "Son, I'm afraid I have some bad news," he began.

David's heart rate shot up immediately. "About Daisy?" he blurted. "Is she okay?"

His father offered a weak smile. "Your sister is okay. This has nothing to do with her. Your mother and I were up all night crunching the numbers, and we just don't have the money for your spring training trip and new uniform this year. I'm sorry."

That meant he couldn't play baseball this season, his last in high school. David knew that the family needed to make sacrifices for Daisy, but he couldn't help but feel angry that he had to give up the one thing he truly loved. David quickly turned away to hide his face. He wanted to shout that this wasn't fair. Hadn't their life changed enough? Didn't they understand that he needed this final season with his team? Was it too much to ask for something for himself for once?

"It's okay," he exhaled as his father left the room.

Skill:
Descriptive Details

Isaiah realizes that he should add descriptive details to help readers picture the setting in this section of his narrative. So he adds details about where and when the conversation takes place.

Skill:
Narrative Techniques

In this section, Isaiah decides to improve the characterization and dialogue and adjust the pacing. He wants readers to feel David's initial panic and understand his reaction to what his dad says.

~~They heard a loud bang and the car came to a stop in the middle of the road. After an expensiver emergency tow and a mechanic's inspection, they learned that the engine would need to be replaced. The same thing happened to one of David's friends last year. The estimate was more than $2000. It was the family's only car. With Daisy's medical bills, they couldn't afford to spend that kind of money on repairs. But without the car, they couldn't take Daisy to get her cancer treatments. He gently placed his arm around his mother's shoulders and gave her a tight squeeze.~~

A month later, as David and his mother were driving home from school, they heard a loud bang and the car came to a stop in the middle of the road. After an expensive emergency tow and a mechanic's inspection, they learned that the engine would need to be replaced. The estimate was more than $2000. It was the family's only car. With Daisy's medical bills, they couldn't afford to spend that kind of money on repairs. But without the car, they couldn't take Daisy to get her cancer treatments. David's guilt over feeling upset about baseball was immediate and crushing. He was wrong to be selfish when his family was counting on him to be strong. He gently placed his arm around his mother's shoulders and gave her a tight squeeze.

"It'll be okay, Mom," she said brightly. "I swear."

Now he just had to find a way to keep that promise.

David has been avoiding his baseball teammates since his unexpected retirement. Stories about preseason practices kept him away from their lunch tables, and it was painful to watch them head off to the field after school. But after three years of playing together, his former teamates were still your best friends and the only people you knew he could count on for help.

The locker room is looking the same as it had the last time David entered it. The harsh overhead lights reflect off the red metal lockers, and the floor was just as mysterious damp as it has always been. He took careful and deliburet steps, pausing only for a moment to glance at the locker that should have been ours. His coach was the first to spot it.

NOTES

⚙ Skill:
Transitions

Isaiah notes that the change in setting and time is unclear in this section. He decides to use transitions to signal a shift in time and place.

"David! I hope this means you're coming back to the team."

"Not quiet, Coach," David could feel everyone staring at him. Sudden shy, he lowers his voice and asks, "Can we talk in your office for a minute?"

David and Coach Warner agree that the team could host a fundraiser to help David's family. Coach and David discussed the details. Coach had barely finished his speech before every team member's hand was in the air. David beamed. The team would host a fundraiser for David's family. He remembered how much fun it was to be part of the team.

The fundraiser was a success. The team raised enough money to pay for the car repairs with a bit left over to cover some of Daisy's medical bills. David's dad was so proud of them. He said to David, You saved the day, son. How does it feel to be a hero?"

~~David is smiling as he thought about everything that has happened. I think I figured out what I want to do with my spare time now that I'm not playing baseball. I found a local organization that helps families who are dealing with childhood cancers, and I am going to help. I'm going to lead the team. We will do a new fundraiser for another family. Coach says he'll help me do a new one next year. I will be home from college for spring break."~~

~~Daisy couldn't hide her excitement. She was proud to have a brother that would help him in this way.~~

Skill:
Conclusions

Isaiah adds dialogue that allows David and Daisy to share their thoughts and feelings. By doing so, Isaiah helps readers better understand the characters and the significance of the events in the story.

David flashed a smile as he thought about everything that had happened. "Don't be silly, Dad. I'm no hero. But I think I figured out what I want to do with my spare time now that I'm not playing baseball. I found a local organization that helps families who are dealing with childhood cancers, and I volunteered to help. I'm going to lead the team on a new fundraiser for another family. Coach says he'll help me do a new one next year when I'm home from college for spring break."

Daisy reached up from her wheelchair and grabbed David's hand. "Say whatever you want, big brother, but you'll always be my hero."

Skill:
Story Beginnings

sync•skills

••• CHECKLIST FOR STORY BEGINNINGS

Before you write the beginning of your narrative, ask yourself the following questions:

- What information does my reader need to know at the beginning of the story about the narrator, main character, setting, and conflict?
- What will happen to my character in the story?
- Should I establish either a single narrator or multiple points of view?

There are many ways to help you engage and orient your reader. Here are some questions and methods to help you present a problem, situation, or observation and its significance, introduce a narrator and/or characters, and establish one or multiple point(s) of view:

- Action

  > What action could help reveal information about my character or conflict?

  > How might an exciting moment or observation and its significance grab my reader's attention?

  > How could a character's reaction help set the mood?

- Description

  > Does my story take place in a special location or specific time period?

  > How can describing a location or character grab my reader's attention? What powerful emotions can I use?

- Dialogue

  > What dialogue would help my reader understand the setting or the conflict?

  > How could a character's internal thoughts provide information for my reader?

- Information

  > Would a surprising statement grab a reader's attention?

> What details will help my reader understand the character, conflict, or setting?

• Point of view

> one point of view: first person or third person—third-person omniscient or third-person limited

> multiple points of view, introducing more than one narrator or character to tell the story

⟳ YOUR TURN

Below is the first paragraph of Isaiah's narrative draft. Choose the best answer to each question about his story beginning.

> David stood next to the hospital bed and watch as Daisy slept. The same question play on a loop in his head, how did this happen again? Daisy was 11 years old now. The cancer had been gone for seven years. David had been studied the topic in its honors biology class, so he understood how cancer cells work. Still, as he looked down at her little sister, he couldn't understand how the lukeamia could come back after all this time.

1. Which line could you add to Isaiah's first paragraph to better show the relationship David has with his sister and establish a stronger conflict?

   ○ A. David is frustrated by the number of hospital personnel in his sister's room.

   ○ B. David is concerned that the doctors have misdiagnosed his sister's cancer.

   ○ C. David notices his sister is shivering as she sleeps and finds a blanket in the closet to wrap around her.

   ○ D. David's coach contacts his parents about quitting the baseball team.

2. How does the last sentence in the paragraph help the reader better understand the main character?

   ○ A. Even though he understands how cancer works, he doesn't want it to be true that the cancer has returned.

   ○ B. The detail "he looked down at" his little sister helps the reader understand that David does not respect his sister.

   ○ C. It provides background information on David's knowledge of cancer.

   ○ D. It tells the reader that his sister has been in remission for years.

✎ WRITE

Use the questions in the checklist to revise the beginning of your narrative.

Skill:
Narrative Techniques

••• CHECKLIST FOR NARRATIVE TECHNIQUES

As you begin to develop the techniques you will use in your narrative, ask yourself the following questions:

- Is it clear which character is talking in a dialogue?

- Is the pacing of events suitable and effective?

- Which literary devices can strengthen descriptions of the characters or plot events? How can I use personal reflection to develop my narrative?

- What additional characters and/or events might help to develop the narrative?

Here are some methods that can help you use dialogue, description, pacing, reflection, and multiple plot lines to develop experiences, events, and/or characters in your narrative:

- use character dialogue to explain events or actions

  > use quotation marks correctly

  > include identifying names as needed before or after quotation marks

- use description so the reader can visualize the characters, setting, and other elements

  > descriptions should contribute to the reader's understanding of the element being described

- use pacing effectively

  > for a quick pace, use limited description, short paragraphs, brief dialogue, and simpler sentences

  > for a slower pace, use detailed description, longer paragraphs, and complex sentence structures

- use reflection to comment on the overall message

  > include a character's or personal inner thoughts or insights

- create multiple plot lines that further develop the narrative's message

  > include characters, events, or other elements that will further develop the plot

- use any combination of the techniques above

Copyright © BookheadEd Learning, LLC

⟳ YOUR TURN

Choose the best answer to each question.

1. Below is a section from a previous draft of Isaiah's story in which the setting is unclear. How should he rewrite the underlined sentence to clarify the setting of the scene?

> <u>David followed Coach Warner into the room and sat down on a chair.</u> He noticed that his palms were starting to sweat. He was nervous.

- ○ A. David followed Coach Warner into his office and sat down on a cold metal folding chair.
- ○ B. David said, "Hi, Coach," before following the man into the room and sitting down on a chair.
- ○ C. David followed Coach Warner, a middle-aged man, into the room and sat down on a chair.
- ○ D. David felt his heart beat faster as he followed Coach Warner into the room and sat down on a chair.

2. Isaiah wants to improve the dialogue in a previous draft of his story. In the excerpt below, what change should he make to improve the dialogue so that it shows the characters' feelings?

> (1) David listened to his parents' conversation. The doctor explained, "The cancer is more aggressive this time."
> (2) David could hear his mother's gasp. Then she said, "Is there anything we can do?"
> (3) "There's an experimental treatment we can try," the doctor stated calmly.
> (4) "We'll do anything!" David's father cried.

- ○ A. Change *explained* to *shouted* in paragraph 1.
- ○ B. Change *said* to *squeaked* in paragraph 2.
- ○ C. Change *stated* to *whispered* in paragraph 3.
- ○ D. Change *cried* to *cheered* in paragraph 4.

✏ WRITE

Use the questions in the checklist for narrative techniques to revise a section of your narrative.

Skill:
Transitions

••• CHECKLIST FOR TRANSITIONS

Before you revise your current draft to include transitions, think about:

- the order of plot events

- how events build to create a unified story, build a specific mood, and work toward a particular outcome

Next, reread your current draft and note areas in your narrative where:

- the order of events is unclear or illogical

- changes in time or setting are confusing or unclear. Look for:

  > sudden jumps

  > missing or illogical plot events or outcome(s)

  > moments where the mood does not connect to the development of plot events

Revise your draft to use a variety of techniques to sequence events so that they build on one another to create a coherent whole and build toward a particular mood and outcome, using the following questions as a guide:

- What other techniques could I use so that events in my story build on one another, creating a coherent whole?

- Does the sequence of events in my story build toward a particular mood and outcome?

  > For example, you can build the mood of your story by creating a sense of mystery or suspense.

  > For example, you can build toward a particular outcome by showing character growth or by developing a resolution.

- Are there better transitional words, phrases, or clauses that I can use to show shifts in time or setting and relationships between experiences and events?

⟳ YOUR TURN

How could Isaiah revise this paragraph from a draft of his narrative to clarify David's feelings and the mood of his story? Choose the best answer to the question.

> Before she came home, David helped turn their home office into a bedroom. He helped his mom organize her room. His dad started working a second job at a 24-hour supermarket to make up for the lost income. Money grew tight. David did his best to stay optimistic, but each time he looked at his sister, he grew more afraid.

- ○ A. Isaiah could add dialogue between the hospital staff and David to clarify David's feelings and the mood of the story.
- ○ B. Isaiah could use phrases like *first* and *secondly* to clarify the feelings David has toward his sister.
- ○ C. Isaiah could compare his sister's current condition to her initial leukemia diagnosis seven years ago.
- ○ D. Isaiah could provide David's internal dialogue or thoughts to clarify his protagonist's feelings and the mood of the story.

⟳ YOUR TURN

Read the paragraph below. Then, using the checklist on the previous page, revise the paragraph in order to strengthen transitions and create a more coherent whole.

Paragraph	Revision
She was at a loss for words, but wanted to speak. It wasn't very often that words did not come to her. The snow fell in clumps. It made her tired just thinking about it all.	

Skill:
Descriptive Details

First, reread the draft of your narrative and identify the following:

- places where descriptive details are needed to convey experiences and events

- vague, general, or overused words and phrases

- places where you want to tell how something looks, sounds, feels, smells, or tastes, such as:

  > experiences

  > events

  > settings

  > characters

Use telling details, sensory language, and precise words and phrases to convey a vivid picture of the experiences, events, setting, and/or characters, using the following questions as a guide:

- What experiences and events do I want to convey in my writing?

- Have I included telling details that help reveal the experiences and events in the story?

- How do I want the characters and setting portrayed?

- How can I use sensory language—or words that appeal to the sense of sight, sound, touch, smell, or taste—so that readers can clearly visualize the experiences, events, setting, and/or characters in my story?

- What can I refine or revise in my word choice to make sure the reader can picture what is taking place?

 **YOUR TURN**

Choose the best answer to each question.

1. Isaiah would like to add a descriptive sound detail to this sentence from a previous draft. Which sentence best adds a sound detail to his sentence?

> David was alone in his room.

- ○ A. David was alone in his room, surrounded by the stench of old sweat socks.
- ○ B. David was alone in his room when the door started to creak open slowly.
- ○ C. David was alone in his room, playing a video game without distractions.
- ○ D. David was alone in his room, too depressed to notice the sunshine streaming through his window.

2. Isaiah wants to add a detail to better establish the setting of part of his story. Which sentence should he add to the excerpt below from a previous draft to help readers visualize the setting?

> The hazy gray sky matched David's mood. The last thing he wanted to do was ask the baseball team for help. He tried to ignore the sounds of laughter coming from their table, but he couldn't.

- ○ A. He needed to catch their attention before the bell rang and he lost his opportunity.
- ○ B. The mouth-watering scent of the tacos they were enjoying made him regret his choice of a peanut butter sandwich.
- ○ C. Their matching uniforms and wide smiles made David ache to be part of the baseball team again.
- ○ D. The cafeteria was teeming with students hanging out with their friends, but David was all alone.

WRITE

Use the questions in the checklist for descriptive details to revise a section of your narrative.

Skill:
Conclusions

••• CHECKLIST FOR CONCLUSIONS

Before you write your conclusion, ask yourself the following questions:

- What important details should I include in my conclusion?

- What other thoughts and feelings could the characters share with readers in the conclusion?

- Should I express the importance of the events in my narrative through dialogue or a character's actions?

Below are two strategies to help you provide a conclusion that follows from and reflects on what is experienced, observed, or resolved over the course of the narrative:

- Peer Discussion

  > After you have written your introduction and body paragraphs, talk with a partner about possible endings for your narrative.

  > Summarize the events in the narrative through the narrator or one of the characters.

  > Describe the narrator's observations about the events they experienced.

  > Reveal to readers why the experiences in the narrative matter through a character's reflections.

  > Write your conclusion.

- Freewriting

  > Freewrite for 10 minutes about what you might include in your conclusion. Don't worry about grammar, punctuation, or having fully formed ideas. The point of freewriting is to discover ideas.

  > Review your notes, and think about how you want to end your story.

  > Summarize the events in the narrative through the narrator or one of the characters.

  > Describe the narrator's observations about the events they experienced.

  > Reveal to readers why the experiences in the narrative matter through a character's reflections.

  > Write your conclusion.

 YOUR TURN

Below are Isaiah's revised concluding paragraphs. Choose the best answer to each question about his conclusion.

> The fundraiser was a success. The team raised enough money to pay for the car repairs with a bit left over to cover some of Daisy's medical bills. That night at the dinner table, David's dad clapped him on the back and said, "You saved the day, son. How does it feel to be a hero?"
>
> David flashed a smile as he thought about everything that had happened. "Don't be silly, Dad. I'm no hero. But I think I figured out what I want to do with my spare time now that I'm not playing baseball. I found a local organization that helps families who are dealing with childhood cancers, and I volunteered to help. I'm going to lead the team on a new fundraiser for another family. Coach says he'll help me do a new one next year when I'm home from college for spring break."
>
> Daisy reached up from her wheelchair and grabbed David's hand. "Say whatever you want, big brother, but you'll always be my hero."

1. What effect does the dialogue have in the conclusion of the story?

   - ○ A. It shows that David and his father have finally come to some sort of agreement.
   - ○ B. It reminds the reader that David and his coach have a strong relationship despite his quitting the baseball team.
   - ○ C. It reveals a father's thoughts about his son and provides a resolution to a family problem.
   - ○ D. It reinforces the theme of family.

2. Which sentence in the revised conclusion best shows what Isaiah learned about writing conclusions?

   - ○ A. "The fundraiser was a success."
   - ○ B. "David flashed a smile as he thought about everything that had happened."
   - ○ C. "I'm going to lead the team on a new fundraiser for another family."
   - ○ D. "Daisy reached up from her wheelchair and grabbed David's hand. 'Say whatever you want, big brother, but you'll always be my hero.'"

✎ WRITE

Use the questions in the checklist for conclusions to revise the ending of your narrative.

Narrative Writing Process: Revise

| PLAN | DRAFT | REVISE | EDIT AND PUBLISH |

You have written a draft of your narrative. You have also received input from your peers about how to improve it. Now you are going to revise your draft.

↩ REVISION GUIDE

Examine your draft to find areas for revision. Keep in mind your purpose and audience as you revise for clarity, development, organization, and style. Use the guide below to help you review:

Review	Revise	Example
Clarity		
Label each piece of dialogue so you know who is speaking. Annotate any places where it is unclear who is speaking.	Use the character's name to show who is speaking, or add description about the speaker.	"David!" Coach Warner boomed. "I hope this means you're coming back to the team."
Development		
Identify moments that develop a distinct conflict. Annotate places where you feel the impact of the conflict is not clear.	Focus on a single event and add descriptive details, such as sounds, visual descriptions, and characters' thoughts and feelings, to show how the conflict impacts the characters.	But without the car, they couldn't take Daisy to get her cancer treatments. David's guilt over feeling upset about baseball was immediate and crushing. He was wrong to be selfish when his family was counting on him to be strong. He gently placed his arm around his mother's shoulders and gave her a tight squeeze.

Review	Revise	Example
Organization		
Explain your story in one or two sentences. Reread and annotate any places that don't match your explanation.	Rewrite the events in the correct sequence. Delete events that are not essential to the story.	Coach had barely finished his speech before every team member's hand was in the air. David beamed. ~~The team would host a fundraiser for David's family. He remembered how much fun it was to be part of the team.~~
Style: Word Choice		
Identify every form of the verb *to be* (*am, is, are, was, were, be, being, been*).	Select sentences to rewrite using action verbs.	"I found a local organization that helps families who are dealing with childhood cancers, and I ~~am going~~ volunteered to help."
Style: Sentence Fluency		
Think about a key event where you want your reader to feel a specific emotion. Long sentences can draw out a moment and make a reader think; short sentences can show urgent actions or danger.	Rewrite a key event making your sentences longer or shorter to achieve the emotion you want your reader to feel.	"I'm going to lead the team. on ~~We will do~~ a new fundraiser for another family. Coach says he'll help me do a new one next year. ~~I will be~~ when I'm home from college for spring break."

✏ WRITE

Use the revision guide, as well as your peer reviews, to help you evaluate your narrative to determine areas that should be revised.

Grammar: Modifiers

Most adjectives and adverbs have three degrees: the positive, or base, form; the comparative form; and the superlative form. The base form cannot be used to make a comparison. The comparative form compares two things. The superlative form compares three or more things.

In general, you can form the comparative by adding -*er* and the superlative by adding -*est*. (In some cases a spelling change is required.)

Comparative	Superlative
Last night when I spoke with you about the fall of Rome, I knew at that moment that troops of the United States and our Allies were crossing the Channel in another and **greater** operation. D-Day Prayer	So far from it, that, after surveying the history of woman, I cannot help agreeing with the **severest** satirist, considering the sex as the weakest as well as the most oppressed half of the species. . . . A Vindication of the Rights of Woman

Use *more* and *most* (or *less* and *least* for the opposite) to form the degrees of comparison in the following situations:

Rule	Example
adverbs that end in -*ly*	Did they murder each other **more gently** because in the woods sweet songbirds sang? Grendel
modifiers of three or more syllables	Perhaps the **most extraordinary** development of all is that Shakespeare's Globe Theater in London—built as a monument for his plays and with aspirations to be a world-class study center—became, under the stewardship of the artistic director Mark Rylance, a kind of clearinghouse for anti-Stratford sentiment. Shakespeare: The World As Stage

↻ YOUR TURN

1. How should this sentence be changed?

> In the 1960s, when *Silent Spring* was published, many people believed that pesticides were safe than the insects they were meant to kill.

- ○ A. In the 1960s, when *Silent Spring* was published, many people believed that pesticides were safest than the insects they were meant to kill.
- ○ B. In the 1960s, when *Silent Spring* was published, many people believed that pesticides were safer than the insects they were meant to kill.
- ○ C. In the 1960s, when *Silent Spring* was published, many people believed that pesticides were more safe than the insects they were meant to kill.
- ○ D. No change needs to be made to this sentence.

2. How should this sentence be changed?

> Birds appeared to be sensitive to the effects of pesticides than other animals.

- ○ A. Birds appeared more to be sensitive to the effects of pesticides than other animals.
- ○ B. Birds appeared to be sensitive to the effects of pesticides rather than other animals.
- ○ C. Birds appeared to be more sensitive to the effects of pesticides than other animals.
- ○ D. No change needs to be made to this sentence.

3. How should this sentence be changed?

> The most powerfully of all these chemicals, DDT was banned in the United States.

- ○ A. The powerfully of all these chemicals, DDT was banned in the United States.
- ○ B. The most powerful of all these chemicals, DDT was banned in the United States.
- ○ C. The most powerfullest of all these chemicals, DDT was banned in the United States.
- ○ D. No change needs to be made to this sentence.

Grammar: Pronoun-Antecedent Agreement

A pronoun is a word that takes the place of a noun mentioned earlier. The noun is the pronoun's antecedent. A pronoun must agree in number, gender, and person with its antecedent.

Sometimes a pronoun has another pronoun as its antecedent. When that is the case, the two pronouns should also agree in person. These pairs of pronouns agree in person: *you/your, he/his, she/her, they/their*.

When the antecedent of a pronoun is a collective noun, such as *class* or *team*, the number of the pronoun depends on whether the collective noun is used as singular or plural. The sentence should make clear that *team*, for example, refers either to individual members of the team or to the team as a single unit.

Text	Pronoun	Antecedent
We hold these truths to be self-evident, that all **men** are created equal, that **they** are endowed by **their** Creator with certain unalienable Rights, that among these are Life, Liberty, and the pursuit of Happiness. The Declaration of Independence	they their	men
When a **woman** has five grown-up daughters **she** ought to give over thinking of **her** own beauty. Pride and Prejudice	she her	woman
Heathcliff had knelt on one knee to embrace her; **he** attempted to rise, but she seized **his** hair, and kept **him** down. Wuthering Heights	he his him	Heathcliff
I take the **world** as I find **it**, in trade and everything else. Middlemarch	it	world

Note that the antecedent should be clear.

Clear	Unclear	Explanation
Park in the garage and lock the **car**.	When you put the car in the garage, don't forget to lock **it**.	The pronoun *it* could refer to either the car or the garage.

↻ YOUR TURN

1. How should this sentence be changed?

> They swam to the far shore where you could find shells.

- ○ A. They swam to the far shore where she could find shells.
- ○ B. They swam to the far shore where it could find shells.
- ○ C. They swam to the far shore where they could find shells.
- ○ D. No change needs to be made to this sentence.

2. How should this sentence be changed?

> Robert Louis Stevenson started traveling to improve his health and soon began writing novels that would leave their impression on millions of readers.

- ○ A. Robert Louis Stevenson started traveling to improve their health and soon began writing novels that would leave their impression on millions of readers.
- ○ B. Robert Louis Stevenson started traveling to improve our health and soon began writing novels that would leave their impression on millions of readers.
- ○ C. Robert Louis Stevenson started traveling to improve his health and soon began writing novels that would leave its impression on millions of readers.
- ○ D. No change needs to be made to this sentence.

3. How should this sentence be changed?

> The class had their first meeting yesterday.

- ○ A. The class had its first meeting yesterday.
- ○ B. The class had your first meeting yesterday.
- ○ C. The class had my first meeting yesterday.
- ○ D. No change needs to be made to this sentence.

4. How should this sentence be changed?

> Since my father enjoyed his birthday party so much, I was glad I had not forgotten it.

- ○ A. Since my father enjoyed his birthday party so much, I was glad I had not forgotten you.
- ○ B. Since my father enjoyed his birthday party so much, I was glad I had not forgotten his birthday.
- ○ C. Since my father enjoyed his birthday party so much, I was glad I had not forgotten.
- ○ D. No change needs to be made to this sentence.

Grammar:
Basic Spelling Rules II

Follow these rules to avoid making some common spelling mistakes.

Rule	Text
If a one-syllable word ends in a single consonant preceded by a single vowel, double the final consonant before adding a suffix that begins with a vowel, such as -ed or -ing.	"Stand up," said Arthur, and he **clapped** his hands for a page to take away the seat. The Once and Future King
Double the final consonant if the last syllable of the word is accented and the accent does not move after the suffix is added.	And I feel that notwithstanding the past that my presence here is one additional bit of evidence that the American Dream need not forever be **deferred**. 1976 Democratic National Convention Keynote Address, by Barbara Jordan
Do not double the final consonant if the last syllable of the word is not accented or if the accent moves when the suffix is added.	Since then, when he had **happened** to see the sun come up in the country or on the water, he had often **remembered** the young Swedish girl and her milking pails. O Pioneers!
Do not double the final consonant if the suffix begins with a consonant. However, when adding -ness to a word that ends in n, keep the n.	I like him not; nor stands it safe with us / To let his **madness** range. Hamlet
Do not double the final consonant when adding suffixes if two vowels come before the final consonant or if the word ends in two consonants.	With **straining** eagerness Catherine gazed towards the entrance of her chamber. Wuthering Heights
When forming compound words, keep the original spelling of both words.	After the **sunsets** and the **dooryards** and the sprinkled streets, . . . The Love Song of J. Alfred Prufrock

Please note that excerpts and passages in the StudySync® library and this workbook are intended as touchstones to generate interest in an author's work. The excerpts and passages do not substitute for the reading of entire texts, and StudySync® strongly recommends that students seek out and purchase the whole literary or informational work in order to experience it as the author intended. Links to online resellers are available in our digital library. In addition, complete works may be ordered through an authorized reseller by filling out and returning to StudySync® the order form enclosed in this workbook.

↻ YOUR TURN

1. How should this sentence be changed?

> After being admited to college, Jerome deferred enrolling for one year so he could work to earn money for tuition.

- ○ A. After being admitted to college, Jerome deferred enrolling for one year so he could work to earn money for tuition.
- ○ B. After being admited to college, Jerome defered enrolling for one year so he could work to earn money for tuition.
- ○ C. After being admited to college, Jerome deferred enroling for one year so he could work to earn money for tuition.
- ○ D. No change needs to be made to this sentence.

2. How should this sentence be changed?

> Fariba was thrilled when she discoverred she had won the coveted scholarship to attend the prestigious university.

- ○ A. Fariba was thriled when she discoverred she had won the coveted scholarship to attend the prestigious university.
- ○ B. Fariba was thrilled when she discovered she had won the coveted scholarship to attend the prestigious university.
- ○ C. Fariba was thrilled when she discoverred she had won the covetted scholarship to attend the prestigious university.
- ○ D. No change needs to be made to this sentence.

3. How should this sentence be changed?

> The busy mom strapped her toddler into the shopping cart at the supermarket and headed down the first aisle.

- ○ A. The busy mom straped her toddler into the shopping cart at the supermarket and headed down the first aisle.
- ○ B. The busy mom strapped her toddler into the shoping cart at the supermarket and headed down the first aisle.
- ○ C. The busy mom strapped her toddler into the shopping cart at the super market and headed down the first aisle.
- ○ D. No change needs to be made to this sentence.

Narrative Writing Process: Edit and Publish

| PLAN | DRAFT | REVISE | EDIT AND PUBLISH |

You have revised your fictional or personal narrative based on your peer feedback and your own examination.

Now, it is time to edit your narrative. When you revised, you focused on the content of your narrative. You probably looked at your story's beginning, narrative techniques, transitions, descriptive details, and conclusion. When you edit, you focus on the mechanics of your story, paying close attention to things like grammar and punctuation.

Use the checklist below to guide you as you edit:

☐ Have I followed all the basic rules for correct spelling?

☐ Do my pronouns and antecedents agree?

☐ Have I used both comparative and superlative modifiers correctly?

☐ Have I used a consistent verb tense throughout the story?

☐ Do I have any sentence fragments or run-on sentences?

Notice some edits Isaiah has made:

- Changed his verb tense to maintain consistency

- Corrected commonly misspelled words

- Changed pronouns to agree with their antecedents

Please note that excerpts and passages in the StudySync® library and this workbook are intended as touchstones to generate interest in an author's work. The excerpts and passages do not substitute for the reading of entire texts, and StudySync® strongly recommends that students seek out and purchase the whole literary or informational work in order to experience it as the author intended. Links to online resellers are available in our digital library. In addition, complete works may be ordered through an authorized reseller by filling out and returning to StudySync® the order form enclosed in this workbook.

Reading & Writing Companion 187

David ~~has~~ had been avoiding his baseball teammates since his unexpected retirement. Stories about preseason practices kept him away from their lunch tables, and it was painful to watch them head off to the field after school. But after three years of playing together, his former ~~teamates~~ teammates were still ~~your~~ his best friends and the only people ~~you~~ he knew he could count on for help.

The locker room ~~is looking~~ looked the same as it had the last time David entered it. The harsh overhead lights ~~reflect~~ reflected off the red metal lockers, and the floor was just as mysteriously damp as it ~~has~~ had always been. He took careful and ~~deliburet~~ deliberate steps, pausing only for a moment to glance at the locker that should have been ~~ours~~ his. His coach was the first to spot ~~it~~ him.

✏ WRITE

Use the questions on the previous page, as well as your peer reviews, to help you evaluate your narrative to determine areas that need editing. Then, edit your narrative to correct those errors.

Once you have made all your corrections, you are ready to publish your work. You can distribute your writing to family and friends, hang it on a bulletin board, or post it on your blog. If you publish online, share the link with your family, friends, and classmates.

The Legend of Carman

FICTION

Introduction

This short story revisits an ancient Irish myth about an Athenian sorceress named Carman and her three sons—Dub, Dother, and Dian. Once Carman sees the fertile green fields of Ireland, she decides to conquer the current rulers, the Tuatha Dé Dannan, and make the land her home, but her sons' bad behavior leads to unforeseen complications.

VOCABULARY

progeny
offspring or children

callous
not sensitive; unsympathetic

usurp
to take power using illegal means

NO
IMAGE
PROVIDED

deplorable
worthy of criticism or regret

treason
the crime of betraying one's country

NOTES

READ

1 Hearken! Attend the tale of noble Carman, the fair. Hold your tongues. Listen closely to her sorrowful story.

2 Carman, the raven-haired warrior woman from Athens, was a wonder. The gods blessed this battle-tested beauty with magic powers. Her three sons, a rank of rapacious offspring, were always with her. Dub, the Black-Hearted, had a soul as dark as the deepest cavern. Dother, the Evil, hated everything. Dian, the Violent, was a walking nightmare, leaving a bevy of victims wherever he traveled. Carman and her sons had been searching for land to conquer when she heard news of skirmishes on the shores of Ireland. Despite her great gifts, she never could have guessed that their next voyage would be her last. Not even her most skillful spell could save her from her sons' selfish mistake.

3 The Tuatha Dé Dannan had recently descended upon Ireland's emerald shores. Their name means "tribe of the gods," and gods they were. The Tuatha Dé Dannan came to the coast of Connemara in clouds of mist. Some

say they sailed into the harbor like men and burned their boats, creating smoke that spread out across the land. Others swear that they came down from the heavens on dark clouds like a fine rain. These supernatural beings brought with them three days and three nights of complete darkness, a harbinger of changes to come. No one knows the true story of how the Tuatha Dé Dannan arrived in Ireland. But everyone knows how they fought their way across the land until it was theirs.

4   Carman saw an opportunity when she heard about the recent unrest. Perhaps she and her power-hungry **progeny** could **usurp** the new leaders. Barely rested from their last battle, they boarded a boat and sailed toward their next conquest.

5   Carman and her sons came upon the southern shore of Ireland in their mighty vessel. She marveled at the green land that lay before them. Countless cattle and crops covered the countryside. She decided that her clan could be content living on that coast. "Soon," she said to the terrible trio, "all you see will be ours." The Black-Hearted, the Evil, and the Violent raised their swords, preparing to take the land by force. But wise and noble Carman knew a better way. She called upon her ancient powers and cast a spell across the land. Her magic turned green to gray. The crops withered away at her words. The soil under the shriveled roots would live to grow plants again, but the Irish would be too weak with hunger to fight. They would need Carman to reverse the spell, so they would welcome her as their queen.

6   But Carman would not succeed. The brothers did not obey their orders. As Carman slept, they laid siege to the nearest village. Their actions drew the attention of the Tuatha Dé Dannan. Before morning, the brothers were captured and given the choice between death or exile. They deserted Carman to save themselves. As punishment for her sons' crimes, fair Carman was sealed in a tomb and buried alive. Her sons' **treason** burned in her chest like a thousand flames. Her cry of grief echoed across the cliffs as breath left her body. Carman's anguish revealed her remorse and reversed her spell. The farms became more bountiful than ever before. The Irish were satisfied by the sorceress's sacrifice.

7   Too late, the Irish realized that Carman was not as **callous** as her sons. Deeply affected by her **deplorable** death and her final act of mercy, the townspeople held a festival in her honor. The land where her brave bones are buried was renamed Carman to pay tribute to this noble woman's memory.

First Read

Read the story. After you read, complete the Think Questions below.

1. Who are the main characters in the story? Include their relationship in your response.

   The main characters are _____.

   Their relationship is _____.

2. Write two or three sentences describing Carman's plan to take the land from the Tuatha Dé Dannan.

   Carman's plan is _____

   _____.

3. Why does Carman fail to take the land from the Tuatha Dé Dannan? Cite a line from the text as evidence.

   Carman fails to take the land because _____

   _____.

4. Use context to confirm the meaning of the word *deplorable* as it is used in "The Legend of Carman." Write your definition of *deplorable* here.

   Deplorable means _____.

   A context clue is _____.

5. What is another way to say that a person is *callous*?

   A person is callous when _____

   _____.

Skill:
Analyzing Expressions

★ DEFINE

When you read, you may find English expressions that you do not know. An **expression** is a group of words that communicates an idea. Three types of expressions are idioms, sayings, and figurative language. They can be difficult to understand because the meanings of the words are different from their **literal**, or usual, meanings.

An **idiom** is an expression that is commonly known among a group of people. For example, "It's raining cats and dogs" means it is raining heavily. **Sayings** are short expressions that contain advice or wisdom. For instance, "Don't count your chickens before they hatch" means do not plan on something good happening before it happens. **Figurative** language is when you describe something by comparing it with something else, either directly (using the words *like* or *as*) or indirectly. For example, "I'm as hungry as a horse" means I'm very hungry. None of the expressions are about actual animals.

••• CHECKLIST FOR ANALYZING EXPRESSIONS

To determine the meaning of an expression, remember the following:

✓ If you find a confusing group of words, it may be an expression. The meaning of words in expressions may not be their literal meaning.

- Ask yourself: Is this confusing because the words are new? Or because the words do not make sense together?

✓ Determining the overall meaning may require that you use one or more of the following:

- context clues

- a dictionary or other resource

- teacher or peer support

✓ Highlight important information before and after the expression to look for clues.

⟳ YOUR TURN

Read the following excerpt from "The Legend of Carman." Then, complete the multiple-choice questions below.

---

from "The Legend of Carman"

But Carman would not succeed. The brothers did not obey their orders. As Carman slept, they laid siege to the nearest village. Their actions drew the attention of the Tuatha Dé Dannan. Before morning, the brothers were captured and given the choice between death or exile. They deserted Carman to save themselves. As punishment for her sons' crimes, fair Carman was sealed in a tomb and buried alive. Her sons' treason burned in her chest like a thousand flames. Her cry of grief echoed across the cliffs as breath left her body. Carman's anguish revealed her remorse and reversed her spell. The farms became more bountiful than ever before. The Irish were satisfied by the sorceress's sacrifice.

---

1. What is the meaning of the expression "Her sons' treason burned in her chest like a thousand flames"?

   ○ A. Carmen is annoyed by her sons' betrayal.

   ○ B. Carman is not affected by her sons' betrayal.

   ○ C. Carman feels physical pain being buried alive.

   ○ D. Carmen feels extreme emotional distress because of her sons' betrayal.

2. A sentence that best supports the correct answer to question 1 is:

   ○ A. "Before morning, the brothers were captured and given the choice between death or exile."

   ○ B. "As punishment for her sons' crimes, fair Carman was sealed in a tomb and buried alive."

   ○ C. "Her cry of grief echoed across the cliffs as breath left her body."

   ○ D. "The farms became more bountiful than ever before."

3. Which phrase best describes the expression featured in question 1?

   ○ A. an idiom

   ○ B. figurative language

   ○ C. literal language

   ○ D. a saying

Skill:
Sharing Information

★ DEFINE

Sharing information involves asking for and giving information. The process of sharing information with other students can help all students learn more and better understand a text or a topic. You can share information when you participate in **brief** discussions or **extended** speaking assignments.

⋯ CHECKLIST FOR SHARING INFORMATION

When you have to speak for an extended period of time, as in a discussion, you ask for and share information. To ask for and share information, you may use the following sentence frames:

✓ To ask for information:

- What do you think about _____?

- Do you agree that _____?

- What is your understanding of _____?

✓ To give information:

- I think _____.

- I agree because _____.

- My understanding is _____.

↻ YOUR TURN

Watch the *We Choose to Go to the Moon* StudySyncTV episode. After watching, sort the following statements from the episode into the chart below. Differentiate between statements that introduce text evidence and statements that express ideas about text evidence.

	Statement Options
A	"He points out that we've got all these great scientists, but there's still so much more to learn."
B	"Yeah. But Kennedy is sending mixed messages."
C	"Kennedy was a competitive guy!"
D	"He was talking about gaining scientific knowledge."
E	"So that's Kennedy's real motivation behind this moon-landing goal."
F	"I think he had other motivations besides gaining scientific knowledge."

Introduces Text Evidence	Expresses Ideas About Text Evidence

Close Read

✏ WRITE

PERSONAL RESPONSE: In "The Legend of Carman," the actions of Carman and her sons lead to Carman's death. Who bears the greatest responsibility for her death? Write a paragraph in which you explain your opinion. Build your case on information from the story. Pay attention to and edit for the spelling rules of suffixes and English spelling patterns.

Use the checklist below to guide you as you write.

☐ Who is most responsible for Carman's death?

☐ Why is that your opinion?

☐ What information from the story supports your opinion?

Use the sentence frames to organize and write your personal response.

In my opinion, _____ (is/are)

responsible for Carman's death. I think so because _____

_____.

Information from the story that supports my opinion includes _____

_____

Carman is put to death because _____

_____.

Long Live King Chazz

FICTION

Introduction

I n this humorous short story, a beloved monarch dies suddenly, and his young, uneducated six-year-old son is forced to take the throne. Once in power, King Chazz acts as any six-year-old might, outlawing bedtimes and broccoli. In the complications that arise during King Chazz's rule, the author offers satirical commentary on contemporary politics and the motivations of political leaders.

V VOCABULARY

succession

the process of replacement for offices, ranks, or titles

competent

able to satisfactorily master and complete a task

welfare

the state of being well, such as being happy, healthy, or successful

delegation

a group of people chosen to represent others and make decisions

factions

small groups that share opinions that are in conflict with a larger group and with one another

≡ READ

— NOTES —

1   A great tragedy occurred one day in the small but majestic kingdom of Abrearia. Our beloved His Royal Highness King Chaderick IV died suddenly of a cold he caught while hunting wild boar in a thunderstorm. His advisers warned him against holding the hunt in such dangerous conditions. But the Annual Wild Boar Hunt has been held on the fourth Sunday after the third full moon in the second season for the past 300 years. He refused to reschedule. It was a terrible loss for our proud nation.

2   However, from even the darkest night arises the brightest sun. King Chaderick's son, His Royal Highness King Chaderick V, has inherited the throne. Stronger than a team of oxen and more brilliant than the brightest diamond, he is truly an awe-inspiring king.

3   Some critics have opposed the rules of **succession** that have allowed King Chazz, as the monarch prefers to be called, to assume the throne at the age of six. But these small-minded complainers fail to see the depths of the king's

Copyright © BookheadEd Learning, LLC

wisdom. Some say he has been ignoring the nation's **welfare** to promote his own agenda. That is not true. For instance, his first official decree made it illegal for anyone to go to sleep before midnight. This was not merely a guise to avoid his own 8 o'clock bedtime. On the contrary, he was showing tremendous selflessness. He sacrificed his own rest so that the nation's engineers, inventors, and musicians could continue their work late into the night without disturbing their sleeping children. Likewise, his second decree outlawed the production and sale of green vegetables. This was not because he himself believes them to be icky. Rather, it is his forward-thinking attempt to inspire the country's farmers to create better-tasting crops. Such efforts will undoubtedly boost trade. What a visionary!

4   Yet, treasonous **factions** have suggested the king might not be the best man for the job. Just because the king has never set foot outside the palace doesn't mean he's out of touch with the people. And just because he doesn't read that well yet doesn't mean he's not capable of writing laws. Luckily for our **competent** leader, our country is governed by divine right. King Chazz was chosen to rule. We would remind any opponents to remember it is our duty to serve our king.

5   Still, those who doubt the king's abilities hounded the palace with protests until King Chazz magnanimously agreed to take on a special adviser. King Chazz set up a **delegation** to look for the sharpest legal minds and most brilliant economists. They visited universities and top corporations. They interviewed distinguished judges and local government officials. They scoured the countryside until they found the best of the best and brought the top candidates to the palace.

6   Every citizen came to witness the king's assessment of these talented individuals. King Chazz lined them up on a stage. Everyone waited to hear the criteria he would use to select the person who would help him run the country. The crowd was abuzz with guesses. Would they have to answer a series of questions or prove their physical strength?

7   King Chazz silenced the crowd and announced that the candidates would participate in a screaming contest. He explained, "For whoever screams the loudest is clearly demonstrating the most passion for our great nation and therefore deserves to hold this important position."

8   One by one, the candidates let out their most ear-piercing cries until tragedy struck a second time. The king's eardrums were indeed pierced. He pulled his too-big crown down to protect his ears, but it was too late. His sense of hearing was lost forever. But this is not a tale of woe. No longer haunted by the criticisms of this earthly realm, King Chazz was finally free to govern as he saw fit. He passed his next royal decree (exiling dentists from the kingdom) without hearing a word of opposition.

First Read

Read the story. After you read, complete the Think Questions below.

☁ **THINK QUESTIONS**

1. What happened to King Chaderick IV? What happened as a result of this event?

   King Chadwick IV _____.

   As a result, _____.

2. What were the first two decrees, or laws, that King Chazz passed after he became king?

   The first decree was _____.

   The second decree was _____.

3. What was King Chazz's plan to choose an adviser? Explain in two or three sentences.

   King Chazz's plan was _____

   _____.

4. Use context to confirm the meaning of the word *delegation* as it is used in "Long Live King Chazz." Write your definition of *delegation* here.

   Delegation means _____.

   A context clue is _____.

5. What is another way to say that King Chazz has been ignoring the nation's *welfare*?

   King Chazz has been ignoring the nation's _____

   _____.

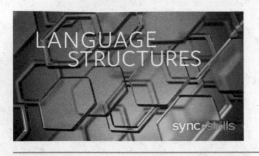

Skill:
Language Structures

★ DEFINE

In every language, there are rules that tell how to **structure** sentences. These rules define the correct order of words. In the English language, for example, a **basic** structure for sentences is subject, verb, and object. Some sentences have more **complicated** structures.

You will encounter both basic and complicated **language structures** in the classroom materials you read. Being familiar with language structures will help you better understand the text.

••• CHECKLIST FOR LANGUAGE STRUCTURES

To improve your comprehension of language structures, do the following:

✓ Monitor your understanding.

- Ask yourself: Why do I not understand this sentence? Is it because I do not understand some of the words? Or is it because I do not understand the way the words are ordered in the sentence?

✓ Break down the sentence into its parts.

- Pay attention to comparatives and superlatives. The **comparative** form compares two things. The **superlative** form compares more than two things.

- Ask yourself: Are there comparatives or superlatives in this sentence? What are they comparing?

✓ Confirm your understanding with a peer or teacher.

↻ YOUR TURN

Read each adjective below. Then, complete the chart by matching each adjective with its comparative and superlative form.

Adjectives				
lighter	softest	most careful	happiest	softer
best	lightest	happier	better	more careful

Adjective	Comparative	Superlative
soft		
careful		
light		
good		
happy		

Skill:
Main Ideas and Details

★ DEFINE

The **main ideas** are the most important ideas of a paragraph, a section, or an entire text. The **supporting details** are details that describe or explain the main ideas.

To **distinguish** between the main ideas and the supporting details, you will need to decide what information is the most important and supports or explains the main ideas.

••• CHECKLIST FOR MAIN IDEA AND DETAILS

In order to distinguish between main ideas and supporting details, do the following:

✓ Preview the text. Look at headings, topic sentences, and boldface vocabulary.

  • Ask yourself: What seem to be the main ideas in this text?

✓ Read the text.

  • Ask yourself: What are the most important ideas? What details support or explain the most important ideas?

✓ Take notes or use a graphic organizer to distinguish between main ideas and supporting details.

↻ YOUR TURN

Read the following from "Long Live King Chazz." Then, complete the multiple-choice questions below.

---

from **"Long Live King Chazz"**

Some critics have opposed the rules of succession that have allowed King Chazz, as the monarch prefers to be called, to assume the throne at the age of six. But these small-minded complainers fail to see the depths of the king's wisdom. Some say he has been ignoring the nation's welfare to promote his own agenda. That is not true. For instance, his first official decree made it illegal for anyone to go to sleep before midnight. This was not merely a guise to avoid his own 8 o'clock bedtime. On the contrary, he was showing tremendous selflessness. He sacrificed his own rest so that the nation's engineers, inventors, and musicians could continue their work late into the night without disturbing their sleeping children. Likewise, his second decree outlawed the production and sale of green vegetables. This was not because he himself believes them to be icky. Rather, it is his forward-thinking attempt to inspire the country's farmers to create better-tasting crops. Such efforts will undoubtedly boost trade. What a visionary!

---

1. What is the main idea of the paragraph?

   ○ A. King Chazz is a child who knows how to make great laws.
   ○ B. Many people support King Chazz's first two laws.
   ○ C. King Chazz's first two laws are so bad that they are actually funny.

2. Which detail best supports the main idea?

   ○ A. "Some critics have opposed the rules of succession..."
   ○ B. "But these small-minded complainers fail to see the depths of the king's wisdom."
   ○ C. "Some say he has been ignoring the nation's welfare to promote his own agenda."

3. Which detail does <u>not</u> support the main idea?

   ○ A. "This was not merely a guise to avoid his own 8 o'clock bedtime. On the contrary, he was showing tremendous selflessness."
   ○ B. "For instance, his first official decree made it illegal for anyone to go to sleep before midnight."
   ○ C. "What a visionary!"

Close Read

✏ WRITE

NARRATIVE: In "Long Live King Chazz," the new king is described as awe-inspiring. Imagine you live in King Chazz's kingdom and that you, in fact, do find him to be an amazing ruler. Write the king a letter and tell him why you find him so awe-inspiring. Provide details from the story that support your main idea. Pay attention to and edit for verb tenses.

Use the checklist below to guide you as you write.

☐ What qualities make King Chazz a good leader?

☐ How do King Chazz's laws help the people in his kingdom?

☐ Which verb tense will you use to write this letter?

Use the sentence frames to organize and write your narrative.

To His Royal Highness King Chazz, I just want to say that I think you are leading our kingdom in the right

direction. No other _____

_____

has the courage to make such _____ policies. For example, your decision to _____

_____

is awe-inspiring. Now, everyone has _____. Our country needs more leaders like you who are

willing to try _____. _____!

Sincerely,

PHOTO/IMAGE CREDITS:

studysync

Text Fulfillment Through StudySync

If you are interested in specific titles, please fill out the form below and we will check availability through our partners.

ORDER DETAILS

Date:

TITLE	AUTHOR	Paperback/ Hardcover	Specific Edition *If Applicable*	Quantity

SHIPPING INFORMATION

Contact:

Title:

School/District:

Address Line 1:

Address Line 2:

Zip or Postal Code:

Phone:

Mobile:

Email:

BILLING INFORMATION ☐ *SAME AS SHIPPING*

Contact:

Title:

School/District:

Address Line 1:

Address Line 2:

Zip or Postal Code:

Phone:

Mobile:

Email:

PAYMENT INFORMATION

☐ CREDIT CARD

Name on Card:

Card Number:

Expiration Date:

Security Code:

☐ PO

Purchase Order Number:

StudySync Text Fulfillment, BookheadEd Learning, LLC
610 Daniel Young Drive | Sonoma, CA 95476